CAN
PUBLIC SCHOOLS
LEARN FROM
PRIVATE SCHOOLS?

**Other books and reports
from the Economic Policy Institute**

*School Choice:
Examining the Evidence*

*Risky Business:
Private Management of Public Schools*

*Where's the Money Gone?
Changes in the Level and Composition
of Education Spending, 1967-91*

*Where's the Money Going?
Changes in the Level and Composition
of Education Spending, 1991-96*

*The Privatization of Public Service:
Lessons From Case Studies*

The Limits of Privatization

http://www.epinet.org

CAN
PUBLIC SCHOOLS
LEARN FROM
PRIVATE SCHOOLS?

CASE STUDIES IN THE PUBLIC & PRIVATE NONPROFIT SECTORS

Richard Rothstein

Martin Carnoy

Luis Benveniste

THE ASPEN INSTITUTE
Nonprofit Sector Research Fund

ECONOMIC POLICY INSTITUTE

The research reported here was supported by the Aspen Institute, with additional support from the Consortium for Policy Research in Education (CPRE), Grant No. OERI-R308A60003. The opinions expressed in this report are those of the authors and do not necessarily reflect the views of the Aspen Institute; the National Institute on Educational Governance, Finance, Policy-Making and Management, Office of Educational Research and Improvement, U.S. Department of Education; or of the institutional partners of CPRE.

Table of contents

Acknowledgments

Several colleagues conducted the case studies upon which this report is based and wrote summaries of their investigations. We have relied on their summaries in writing this report, but interpretations of their conclusions are often our own. We are grateful for their participation in this project; the three co-authors assume sole responsibility for these interpretations (or misinterpretations). Each of these colleagues is identified in the appendix, along with a description of the case or cases for which he or she assumed primary responsibility.

This report benefited from reviews and comments by Richard Elmore, Susan Fuhrman, Eric Hanushek, and Henry Levin. We thank them as well for their assistance, but assure readers that any errors are those of the co-authors alone.

Finally, we are deeply grateful to the principals, teachers, parents, students, and administrators of each of the schools described in this report. They were unfailingly generous with their time and interest, and were surprisingly understanding of our inability, owing to our commitments to interviewees regarding confidentiality, to share in detail all our findings about particular schools. The case study summaries on which this report is based might well have been more accurate if we could have reviewed them with our interview subjects, but this would necessarily have violated the promises of confidentiality we made to each of them. This is another reason why any errors are solely the authors' responsibility.

Executive summary

Because private schools can select (and are selected by) their students, analysts have not been able to determine whether private schools' apparently superior outcomes (like test scores) are attributable to superior private school practices or to more selective student bodies. If superior private school practices are responsible, these practices are widely believed to include more accountability to parents, more clearly defined outcome expectations, a greater clarity of emphasis on both academic and behavioral/value objectives, and more efficient teacher selection and retention policies. Private schools mostly utilize the same curricular materials as public schools, and so private schools' apparently superior outcomes should be able to inspire competing public schools to improve by imitating private school practices.

To explore these widespread beliefs about differences between private and public school practices, we conducted case studies of eight public and eight private elementary schools in California. We conducted extensive interviews with principals, other administrators, teachers, parents, and (in the case of some eighth graders) students. The schools were selected to typify a range of socioeconomic characteristics and included both sectarian and nonsectarian private schools. However, we make no claim that the sample of schools was scientifically chosen, or that the impressions we record here are statistically valid. The depth with which we probed each of these schools precluded a large enough sample to generate statistical conclusions.

Nonetheless, insights from these case studies tend to challenge widely held assumptions about differences between public and private schools. Inner-city private schools shared more characteristics with public schools in low-income communities than with affluent suburban private schools. Likewise, suburban public schools had more in common with suburban private schools than with urban public schools. Thus, policy debates about education may be missing the most important issues if they focus on whether a school's quality can be deduced from its public or private charter. The most important variations between schools may be between schools of all types in different communities, not between public and private schools in the same community.

Among the 16 schools in this sample, private schools were not noticeably more accountable to parents than public schools. In low-income schools, public and private, teachers and administrators complained of the lack of parental involvement. Both public and private school teachers in these low-income communities felt challenged to involve parents even in a minimal way in their children's education (for example, by supervising homework or attending school meetings). And in no sense did we observe either public or private schools in low-income communities acting as though they were "accountable" to parents. But an opposite phenomenon characterized both public and private schools in very affluent communities: here, staff in both types of schools complained of too much parent involvement – including interference in the daily curriculum and inappropriate challenges to school goals.

Policy makers often posit that private schools are more successfully organized around academic achievement objectives and are more successful in emphasizing behavioral goals. These case studies, however, include private schools organized around principles other than academic outcomes, such as religious beliefs, safety, or discipline; in some cases, academic achievement was a relatively low priority. The studies also found some public schools that were as successful as private ones in aligning themselves with academic goals, and some public schools that also emphasized behavioral or value objectives.

Many believe that an important public-private difference is laxity of teacher standards stimulated by public employee protections and unionization. Yet these case studies found no school, public or private, where formal evaluation, supervision, or mentoring of teachers was meaningful. Indeed, Catholic school procedures for terminating poorly performing teachers were nearly as cumbersome as public school procedures. Moreover, private schools in this sample were no more selective in teacher personnel policies than were public schools serving students of similar socioeconomic backgrounds. We observed both high- and low-quality classroom management and academic instruction in both public and private schools.

The social, cultural, and economic backgrounds of the parents and the community in which the school was located seemed to be the main determinant of variation, much more so than a school's public or private character or, within the latter group, whether it was religious or secular. Within particular communities, similarities between schools and the problems they confronted overwhelmed the differences.

These cases point away from arguments that public schools can improve by adopting the greater accountability to parents and flexibility in hiring/firing teachers presumably characteristic of private schools. These may be good policies for all schools to follow, but public schools are as likely (or unlikely) to be accountable to parents as private schools serving similar student and parent populations. These observations, if confirmed by observations of a much broader group of schools, could have important implications for those who champion "choice" in public education as the basis for improving academic achievement. A much greater complexity of factors must be considered when developing "fixes" for our nation's schools.

Introduction

Private school outcomes are generally superior to public school outcomes. Private school students score higher on standardized tests than do public school students, and private school students are more likely to graduate and attend college.

But why is this the case? Do private school practices differ from practices of public schools? Or do private schools get better outcomes because they enroll students from more advantaged backgrounds? Even if private schools generate superior outcomes when student background characteristics are controlled, are these outcomes caused by practices that are transferable to public schools, or are they idiosyncratic to private schooling? For example, improved outcomes for disadvantaged students in private schools that spring from their association with more advantaged classmates would not be a transferable private school effect. Similarly, a private school advantage that derives from a sense of religious community or shared communal values may not be transferable to a secular public school.

Scholars differ on whether private schools *should* behave differently than public schools. Sociologists Richard Scott and John Meyer (1988) argue that the institution of public schooling has a different function than that of a private school, and so the two should have different organizational structures. A public school takes in all comers. Teachers and the school principal are accountable to multiple constituencies, represented by the varying capabilities of their students and their needs. Thus, a public school's organization is bound to be complex and often subject to conflict. It also can appear incoherent because it tries to do so many things at once. Private schools are more likely to have a single objective, and select (and be selected by) the parents and their children who are in accord with that objective. A private school's organization should therefore be less complex — more "aligned" around a coherent program. Sociologist Joan Talbert (1988) also argues for significant organizational differences between public, religious private, and nonreligious private schools on similar grounds.

But economist Byron Brown (1992) theorizes that private and public schools should not differ significantly. Because private and public schools and parents are all generally uncertain about children's abilities and future employment prospects, he argues, they offer comprehensive curricula and similar teaching methods in order to reduce the uncertainty about schooling choices. If a school chooses to differ radically from other schools, it increases the risk to parents that they have made the wrong choice. Whether by voice or exit, parents will push the school to behave much like other schools. Private schools tend to distinguish themselves, Brown concludes, not by innovating academically but by offering special "secondary services," such as religious instruction, that do not affect labor market opportunities.

Much of the debate around differences between nonprofit public and private schools has revolved around statistical analyses that purport to control for student background characteristics, thus leading to the identification of a private school effect that demands explanation. Some scholars (e.g., Coleman, Hoffer, and Kilgore 1982; Peterson 1998) find that students in private schools score higher on achievement tests, even after student backgrounds are taken into account. Others (e.g., Witte 1996; Rouse 1997), however, find little or no private school effect after controlling for student background characteristics.

Because controls for background characteristics are so difficult to implement, it is unlikely that this debate will soon be resolved. Yet public policy does not wait for econometricians to achieve consensus. Controversy regarding the relative advantages of public or private schooling proceeds, and policies to shift resources from public to private schools, based on assumptions about private school superiority, gain increasing support. Ethnographic data may help shed light on this debate by giving us the opportunity to study in detail the principles and practices around which schools organize themselves.

In the pages that follow, we report on case studies of eight public and eight private elementary schools in California.[1] One critique of a study that uses cases, rather than a large random sample of schools, is that it is not necessarily representative and hence cannot yield reliable conclusions regarding possible differences or similarities between private and public schools. It is true that our sample is neither random nor large, but the small number we chose to work with enabled us to observe instruction in classrooms and interview teachers, administrators, and parents. Time and resources did not permit such an observational and interview-based case study approach for more than 16 schools. And 16 is too few a number of schools to assure a representative sample had we selected it randomly. Schools also have too many varying characteristics to assure a representative sample of 16 if we had stratified all public and private schools prior to randomization.

Rather, we drew the sample to mirror the characteristics of important types of schools that might shed light on how nonprofit public and private schools differ. Private schools in our sample include both parochial and independent schools. Public schools include both neighborhood and "choice" (or charter) schools. We also targeted schools within each nonprofit sector (private or public) that served different social class populations (poor, working class, middle income, and affluent) and that varied by urbanicity and racial composition. We believe, despite the nonrepresentative character of the sample, that by visiting a reasonable number of public and private schools in two major metropolitan areas — schools catering to students of varied racial and ethnic backgrounds and from families both higher and lower in socioeconomic characteristics — we should be able to find differences. The widely repeated claim, after all, is that market-driven behavior is *observably* and *significantly* different from bureaucratically driven behavior. If that is the case, such differences should be observable in a sample of 16 schools.

Because interview respondents were assured anonymity, we use pseudonyms as school names, and we do not specify the California community in which each school is located. Appendix A provides a brief description of each school studied, along with a table that classifies each school both by the socioeconomic level of its clientele and by type, i.e., private-religious, private-nonsectarian, private-proprietary/for profit, public-neighborhood, or public-choice. The reader should refer to Appendix A when considering each of the sections below.

Our interviews were organized around a relatively simple working theory of school accountability.[2] It assumes that schools actually have conceptions of accountability embedded in the patterns of their day-to-day operations, and that a school's conception of accountability significantly influences how it delivers education. We expect that schools must solve problems of accountability in some way in order to function, and that how schools solve them is reflected in the way teachers, administrators, students, and parents talk about the fundamental issues of schooling. Schools are likely to have more "operative" internal accountability systems if their formal and informal mechanisms are aligned with individuals' internalized notions of accountability (responsibility) and collective expectations of the school. In schools at the other extreme, there may be a high degree of incoherence among formal and informal mechanisms and individual notions, leading to a relatively weak or even dysfunctional internal accountability system.[3]

We make no effort to draw conclusions from our case studies about the relative effectiveness of the schools we studied, and we did not select the schools to be statistically representative of broader school groupings. Rather, our purpose is descriptive and suggestive: we attempt to identify the practices in each of these schools that we believe may be typical of other schools; our findings could be tested in a larger sample in an effort to confirm a series of hypotheses about what public schools can learn from private schools. We did not attempt to quantify our observations or subject them to statistical analyses; our "tests" of these hypotheses in this very small sample, therefore, are based on interpretations of interviews and personal observations in classrooms and schools, not on quantitative data. This report, then, contributes to the discussion engendered by scholars like Chubb and Moe (1990) (who concluded from observational studies that private school effectiveness is the result of organizational factors — freedom from democratic/bureaucratic control) or Bryk, Lee, and Holland (1993) (who concluded from observational studies that the effectiveness of Catholic schools is the result of a shared sense of communal mission), without first proposing a statistical claim that public or private schools are superior.

Our most striking finding from these cases is that, to the extent patterns are generalizable, the most important distinctions among these schools did not separate public from private institutions. Rather, we found, for example, that private schools in inner-city communities were more similar in many respects to public schools in these communities than they were to private schools in suburban communities. Likewise, we found that the suburban public schools we observed had more in common in many respects with suburban private schools than they had with urban public schools. While these patterns were not uniform, they suggest that policy debates about education may be missing the most important issues if they focus on whether the quality of schools can be deduced from their public or private organization.

In sum, our answer to the question, "what can public schools learn from the private non-profit education sector?" is "not much." But if phrased somewhat differently, i.e., "what can schools, public and private, learn from other schools, public and private," our answer is "quite a bit," depending on which schools we study and what we are attempting to learn.

We came to this conclusion by organizing our observations around the following commonly held generalizations about the superiority of non-profit private schools:

Generalization No. 1: Private elementary school personnel tend to be more accountable to parents than are public elementary school personnel.

Generalization No. 2: Private school outputs and expectations for students tend to be more clearly defined than are public school outputs and expectations.

Generalization No. 3: Private elementary schools tend to produce higher nonachievement outputs — behavior and values, for example — than do public elementary schools. Moreover, private schools allocate a higher proportion of resources to these nonacademic objectives than do public schools.

Generalization No. 4: Teacher selection and retention practices at private schools are more efficient than are the selection and retention practices for teachers at public schools.

Generalization No. 5: Private schools' academic success is accomplished with curricular materials that are not significantly different (in standard subjects) from curricular materials found in public schools.

Generalization No. 6: Private school innovations stimulate improved practices at the public schools with which they compete.

With respect to each of these generalizations about the superiority of private over public schools, our interviews and observations suggest differences between the schools we observed, but the differences did not arrange themselves along a public-private divide. Rather, we found both public and private schools that had greater or lesser parent accountability, more or less well-defined expectations and student outcome goals, more or less emphasis on nonacademic goals, traditional or less traditional curricular materials, more or less rigorous teacher selection and retention policies. We found evidence that schools learn from each other, whether they are public or private.

We discuss our observations with regard to each of these generalizations in turn.

Chapter 1

Accountability to Parents

The first generalization we examined was that *private elementary school personnel tend to be more accountable to parents than are public elementary school personnel.* This notion relies on an expectation that private schools must cater to parents who, if unsatisfied, can and will search for services elsewhere. Public schools, by contrast, have a captive clientele whose only recourse requires the ability and willingness to make significant investments in private education.

We indeed found considerable variation among schools in the degree to which parents were involved, informed, and heeded in the schooling process. Some schools we observed were very accountable to parents and others not at all so. These differences, however, did not seem to be a function of private vs. public education. Rather, the social class of the parents seemed to be a better predictor of schools' accountability than the schools' public-private character. Is this because wealthier parents, with many options, can threaten to leave a school, whether in the public or private sector, if that school is not more accountable to them? Or is it because private schools' accountability systems are not very different from those of public schools? These case studies suggest the latter explanation, but so small a sample cannot prove this proposition with certainty.

Closely connected to patterns of accountability to parents is the extent to which parents are involved in the schooling process. Parental participation in a child's education is usually considered a key element for making high student achievement possible. Education is a joint production that requires mutual support and reinforcement from teachers and parents.

Our studies reveal that, in some schools, instructional staff perceive their greatest problem to be lack of parental involvement in their children's education. Administrators and principals complained frequently that too few parents volunteered in classrooms, that too few parents attended meetings to discuss school policy or to review children's work, and that parents paid insufficient attention to the importance of homework. Schools where these complaints were frequent were low-income schools, both public and private. Low-income private schools[4] have an advantage in procuring parental involvement because they can make it a condition for student enrollment — e.g., parents can be required to sign a "contract" that specifies they will volunteer a certain number of hours per month in the school. At several low-income private schools we observed, however, while great effort was expended to attempt to increase parental participation, this effort was mostly directed to enlisting parents in fundraising endeavors and only secondarily to getting them involved in academic activities.

In other schools, however, we found that administrators and teachers had the opposite complaint: too much parent involvement. In these cases, school faculty argued that parents interfered too frequently in curricular matters, that they had uninformed preconceptions about proper pedagogical or disciplinary practice, and that they exhibited a lack of respect for the professional competence of the instructional staff. This tended to be the case in both private and public schools that served higher-income populations, where parents felt confident that they knew best what a proper education entailed and were without compunction to communicate this to teachers and administrative staff.

Examples of excessive parental involvement were most poignant in two public schools where parents were highly educated professionals who felt strongly about their right to participate in their children's education. For instance, a teacher in an affluent suburban public school said that she typically receives a letter from the parent of *every* child in her class *each* week, with questions or suggestions about her teaching. And an instructor from a public charter school reported that, on her first day of teaching, 25 parents visited her classroom with specific suggestions about how the curriculum ought to be organized. In some private schools in our sample with similarly affluent populations, however, administrators were more successful in resisting parents and insulating teachers from unreasonable parental demands. In these cases, administrators advised parents that curricular and pedagogical decisions were the exclusive prerogative of the school's professional staff. These schools, unlike lower-income private schools we observed, were sufficiently stable financially and had a large enough applicant pool to feel they could afford to alienate some meddlesome purchasers of their product.

Resistance to parents at public Tatuna Point, Olympic Charter, and Adams Charter Middle School

At Tatuna Point, a neighborhood public elementary school in an affluent neighborhood of professionals and executives, there is no shortage of parents who volunteer to work in classrooms, shelve books in the library, staff the computer lab, or direct a variety of extracurricular sports, art, and music programs. Most classrooms, and especially those in the lower grades, have daily parental visitors who work with children in small groups for reading and math, correct spelling tests, or otherwise assist. Parent volunteers also take permanent responsibility for some school-wide clerical duties.

But participation also extends to parents' willingness to criticize instruction. An important share of the principal's time is spent not only responding to parents but defending teachers from parental demands for curricular and instructional changes. An important theme of our interviews with teachers was resentment of what teachers regard as excessive and inappropriate parental interference. Although this "interference" was not characteristic of most parents, a significant minority of vocal and influential parents succeeded in setting the tone for the rest of the school through their participation in the parent-teacher association and other school committees.

Tatuna Point has three separate parent advisory boards, with extensive participation in each. One council raises funds used to hire additional teachers and aides, and parents are especially insistent that these staff, for whom they pay, be deployed as the parent council sees fit. Many parents, for example, have demanded that these classroom aides be used to assist in instruction to reduce the pupil-teacher ratio, while teachers, especially in the upper grades, find it more valuable to have aides relieve them of clerical and organizational tasks so that teachers can have more individual student contact for instruction. This was an ongoing source of conflict.

Parental questioning of school and classroom management has become so extensive that the school established an ombudsman team that organizes and researches parent complaints and publishes summaries in a weekly school bulletin. Complaints typically range from how much protein or how many preservatives school lunch items contain, to the safety of playground equipment, to whether enough homework has been assigned in a particular class, to whether a teacher has progressed far enough in the social studies curriculum, to whether fractions are properly sequenced in the arithmetic curriculum.

Yet this is not a troubled school; on the contrary, test scores average above the 90th percentile in all subjects. The parents seem to believe, though, that this is not good enough, and that the school's failure to do a better job threatens their children's chances for admission to elite colleges. Many parents' concerns are focused on a belief that their children are being held back by other children, purportedly less prepared. Major sources of controversy at the school are widespread parental demands for a tracking system (the teachers resist this) and demands by individual parents that their children be retested if they are not in the upper 2% who statutorily qualify for a "gifted and talented" enrichment program. Because parents are organizationally skilled and articulate, they don't hesitate to appeal to the district superintendent any decision with which they are dissatisfied.

Many teachers find the parental pressure to be so stressful that they remain only a brief time at Tatuna Point before requesting transfers to other district schools. Of the school's 24 teachers, only five have more than four years' tenure at Tatuna Point, a school that, to most outside observers, would seem a desirable place to teach because of its high test scores, affluent student body, and supplementary parent-donated resources.

Like Tatuna Point, the Olympic Charter School also benefits from legions of parent volunteers who assist in classrooms, teach units in their specialties, and take responsibility for office administrative duties. Olympic distinguishes itself by its "constructivist" pedagogical philosophy, defined by one teacher as "an environment where children can create or construct their own learning...with 'hands-on' activities." With roots in Deweyan progressivism and in the "free" or "open school" movement of the 1960-70s, the school selects teachers, and parents select the school, based on adherence to this philosophy.

Despite this explicit self-identification, however — which all parents understand before selecting the school — teachers report that their greatest challenge is to defend the school's pedagogical orientation against demands for greater emphasis on basic skills — demands coming from middle-class parents hoping that more focus on basic skills will gain their children higher scores on standardized tests. One teacher recounted to us that she had increased the importance of memorization of multiplication tables in her curriculum, a change she described as "pacifying the parents." In other cases, however, teachers resist this pressure. One described a year-long dispute with a parent about the teacher's tolerance of spelling errors in a second grader's creative writing; finally, the teacher told the parent, "you can correct your child's spelling at home, but we're not going to do it."

There are other parents who are more ideologically committed to the school's constructivist mission, and, for them, opportunities for holding the school accountable to that mission are plentiful. The principal of the school was hired after a group interview by 32 teachers and parents, following which a consensus was reached.

From the perspective of Olympic's faculty and parent leaders, conflict with parents who cannot accept the school's offbeat style is resolved, ideally, not when the school accommodates itself to parental demands but rather when the school has communicated its philosophy so unequivocally that parents withdraw their children once they become convinced that the school will not meet their objectives. We learned of several cases in which this occurred – i.e., rather than attempt to change the school, parents withdrew their children. Because Olympic's pedagogy emphasizes student choices, not teacher-imposed structure, classrooms can seem chaotic, and children who, by personality, need more order or structure may not do well. Because the character of the school was so explicitly defined, several parents we interviewed understood that they should transfer their children to more traditional schools where needed structure was provided — in one case, the parents kept another sibling, who had greater decision-making ability, at the Olympic Charter School. In addition, we interviewed two Olympic Charter teachers who shared similar personal experiences: each placed one child at Olympic Charter, because she believed the child had the self-motivation to be successful in the relatively unstructured classroom environment, and placed another child at a traditional school.

But while some parents withdraw if the school does not meet their needs, others attempt to change it. Two years ago, there were so many parent complaints about curricular matters that the teachers rebelled and, as a result, Olympic's governing structure was revised: the charter's parent majority on the governing board was replaced with a teacher majority. According to the principal, "teachers want to maintain the stance that the curriculum really is theirs. Ownership. They own the curriculum, and they don't want the parents to have the feeling they can interfere."

We also found a developing tension between parental involvement and over-involvement at Adams Charter Middle School, a small-town public charter school that enrolls only 75 seventh- and eighth-grade students. Like Olympic Charter, it is under the direct jurisdiction of the local school district and receives most of its financing from public funds; but, in many respects, Adams Charter functions more like a private than a public school. It does not accept bilingual or special education students, and it screens other applicants for academic fit before acceptance. While there is no formal tuition, there is a minimum monthly "pledge" and other mandatory requirements for parent participation and fundraising. At Adams, children cannot enroll unless their parents commit to eight hours of volunteer service in the school per month, a requirement they can also fulfill by substituting an additional financial contribution (in excess of the standard minimum monthly pledge of $85) or by purchasing "scrip" in excess of the monthly requirement of $200.[5]

Adams Charter parents participate actively in school activities in fulfillment of their volunteer requirements. There are almost always parents assisting in classrooms and performing other duties, such as running the physical education program for which there is no teacher assigned. This pervasive constructive presence of parents in educational matters gives Adams its most distinctive character. Parental over-involvement in the academic program, however, is also now beginning to be perceived by the faculty as an important concern.

Adams Charter was founded by parents who had previously home-schooled their children. The parents and founding teachers sought charter status because they could access public funds to design a school with a distinctive curricular model focused on the arts. The school building is a converted arts gallery, and student art work is displayed throughout. An artist was a school founder (he remains a teacher at the school), and the school attempts to use the arts to integrate the entire curriculum — "not just the art for the art's sake, but the creative thinking that happens when you get to know art and be involved in art and creativity," according to a parent leader.

Yet despite the curricular vision of the founders, the governing board (where parents are a majority) and other parents recently pressured the staff to add algebra to the eighth-grade curriculum, over the objections of teachers. As a board member recounts, "we did not have an algebra class in place, and if it had been left up to the principal and the teachers, or specifically the math teachers, we probably wouldn't have had an algebra class. But there was a group of us who felt very strongly about offering algebra, and we pushed it through. And so, we have algebra."

Like the principal of Olympic Charter, the principal of Adams Charter now worries that this level of parental interference will become a more common phenomenon and that parents will start "second guessing every aspect of the curriculum." If parents become this involved, the principal says, the school "will have chaos." It has not reached that point, because there remains a shared sense of values and commitment on the part of the small group of parents who founded and support the school. But this charter school of only 75 students may be unable to preserve permanently its idiosyncratic focus; if too many more parents with conventional academic aspirations enroll their children, the unique curriculum of Adams may be lost.

As leaders of public school charters, administrators and faculties of Olympic and Adams attempt to discourage the enrollment of children whose parents do not subscribe to the school's self-defined mission. But this process must be subtle, as the law does not permit public charters to exclude children on philosophical grounds. As we discuss in the following section, a requirement for philosophical compatibility is oftentimes a feature of private education, where schools offer a self-defined product and parents either accept it or withdraw. A very opposite, neighborhood public school style is illustrated by Tatuna Point, a school where parents feel they have a right to shape and influence their community school and where the school feels an obligation to address and respond to parental demands. Because the model of parent-consumer sovereignty is often held up as an ideal for educational reform, Tatuna Point gives policy makers and educators a distinct reality check of what occurs when parents are both self-confident and engaged. A coherent vision of the curriculum or better teaching are not necessarily automatic outcomes of external parental pressures. Schools and districts still need to develop means to make participation useful.

Resistance to parents at private Shalom Ieladim Jewish School

We found similar tensions at the private Shalom Ieladim Jewish School, whose principal also complains that his primary problem is fending off the "meddling" of affluent and highly educated parents in daily curricular matters. As one board member reported with some annoyance, "the school does not exist to serve parents. The school exists to deliver excellent education to families, and it takes more than the parents' view to accomplish that." A teacher explained her view that parents felt they had a right to interfere in daily curricular matters because they were paying substantial tuition and fees ($7,000 per year).

The school is located in an affluent community in which the public schools are widely considered to be of high quality and send large number of graduates on to elite colleges. Parents send their children to Shalom Ieladim not from dissatisfaction with the public schools but rather to obtain a Jewish cultural and religious education in addition to an academic one. The faculty has designed a high-quality general education program that broadly follows the state's curricular frameworks, but not rigidly so. Teachers are permitted and encouraged to emphasize areas of their particular interest — the second-grade teacher focuses on science, while the third-grade teacher focuses on poetry — and constructivist teaching philosophy permeates the school.

Shalom Ieladim urges parents to supervise the performance of homework (but not to participate in its substance), and parents are required to perform 25 hours a year of "volunteer" work in the school (or pay an additional fee of $25 per hour not worked). Parental participation in classrooms is frequent and customary. But while the school welcomes parent involvement in classrooms, parents are not welcomed to decide what will be taught or how — the teacher is the boss. At the Olympic Charter School, on the other hand, parents are not only expected to assist in the classroom, but they need not make appointments to do so; parents can simply show up (and often do), and they are assigned by teachers to work with individual groups of students on whatever project children are then engaged or to lead children in an activity in which the parent is interested or expert, even if this activity might not otherwise have been planned by the teacher. The high socioeconomic and educational level of Olympic parents means that many have academic or artistic skills that can easily be exploited, and the flexible curriculum can adapt to what parents have to offer. At Shalom Ieladim, parents are equally well-educated, but the school is more committed to permitting teachers to vary the curriculum based on their own interests, not those of parents.

At Shalom Ieladim, parental voice does indeed carry a significant weight in school matters; after all, the board that makes all school policy determinations is composed largely of parents. This is a school that operates within a community center and whose primary mission is to serve the community. Parental involvement, nonetheless, does not cross over into academic matters: pedagogical and curricular decisions are the prerogative of the school's professional staff. In describing his resistance to parent interference in the curriculum, the principal of Shalom Ieladim insisted that "this school is not a cooperative."

But the private Shalom Ieladim may still find it somewhat necessary to accommodate its academic program to parental pressures. Like the parents at Tatuna Point and Olympic — all of whom have ambitions for elite college admission for their children — the parents at Shalom Ieladim focus their demands on their schools' achievement credentials. Last year, parents on the school board, supported by other parents and the principal, successfully insisted that the school become accredited, requiring the introduction of standardized testing. Shalom Ieladim's teachers are unhappy about this development. They are concerned that it will change the curricular focus of the school because students will be appraised on standardized tests, rather than by portfolios and more qualitative measures, and their performance will be compared to that of students in the area's public schools. Parents, however, believe it is important to adopt standard parameters that can legitimate their school as a center of high educational quality, comparable to their community's highly regarded public schools.

Structural limits to parent accountability: the Liniers French School's national curriculum and proprietary ownership at Knuckleborough Private School

Parents at the Liniers French School face an even more rigid limit to their ability to propose changes than do parents at Shalom Ieladim or at other private schools with similarly affluent student populations. This private elementary school, serving French-national and American bilingual families of highly educated engineers, scientists, and other professionals, has a tuition rate of $9,500 a year for a program that is not only preparatory for American secondary schools but is also accredited by the French government to deliver the standard French elementary school curriculum. The school has many more applicants than places, and it uses a screening process to ensure that the parents of children who are accepted fully understand the particular characteristics of this school's practices, curriculum, and standards before they enroll.

The school does not intend to bend to parent wishes, and in any case rigid French government curricular requirements would prevent it from doing so. The school's recruitment strategy specifically aims at parents who are willing to accept the curriculum as it is. If parents are dissatisfied about the program of study, they are usually advised that Liniers must not be the school for them. The administration deliberately attempts to recruit as many applicants for a limited number of seats as possible in order to establish Liniers French as a highly selective school and to be able to choose only those parents who fully buy into the school's culture and methods.

Liniers French School faces a variety of challenges to keep parents, whose objectives differ, satisfied. On one hand, a potential danger for the school is that parents of children who will eventually attend secondary school in France will become dissatisfied with time spent on English lessons that detract from preparation for French secondary school admission exams. On the other hand, parents of American children may become dissatisfied with time spent in non-English classes that do not prepare their children eventually for the College Board's SAT. In order to address these tensions, the school administration and teachers have frequent contact with parents to discuss the value of the compromises made to pursue two distinct curricula simultaneously.

Unlike Shalom Ieladim, Liniers French School's strong resistance to parental influence on policy is paired with significant demands for parental involvement in the school's fixed and well-defined instructional program.

The school assures students full bilingualism and preparation for both French and American secondary schools, but there are not enough school hours in the day to accomplish this ambitious goal. The support of parents is indispensable to fulfill the school's curricular objectives.

The parents, all of whom are highly educated, are expected to spend substantial time with children on homework each day to guarantee that the full curriculum can be covered. All student work is sent home weekly, and some teachers require parents to sign it. Parents of children in the lower grades are also expected to volunteer frequently in the school during the instructional day. It might be said, therefore, that Liniers French has partially turned the table around: although the school is accountable to parents for delivering student achievement on its own terms, with no interference by parents in the method it uses to do so, parents are also highly accountable to the school for their children's learning.

That a standardized curriculum restricts a school's accountability to parents is underscored by the fact that Liniers French School's American parents do have some ability to influence the English curriculum, as opposed to their French counterparts who have none. Last year, for example, American parents complained that the first-grade English curriculum was too disorganized and lightweight for their children. This year, the school moved the first-grade teacher to kindergarten, and a new first-grade teacher was hired with specific instructions to increase academic content, with more project work and more emphasis on writing. A similar response to parental pressure would not be possible in the French curriculum, which is specified in detail by French government regulations.

Knuckleborough Private School, a for-profit private school with a predominantly middle- to lower-middle-income student body in a large California city, falls into a category all its own because of the explicitness with which the school's accountability to parents is restricted to "caveat emptor." The proprietors have maintained a clear policy of discouraging parental involvement to prevent interference in the school's operation. Until recently, and for most of the school's 28-year existence, there has been no parent association or other parent advisory group, and no invitations for parents to assist in classrooms. In the last year, the proprietor gave in to parental pressure and permitted an advisory group to form, but she is reluctant to permit it to become too involved in the school's operations.

In part, this slight weakening of the proprietor's resolve is due to growing financial pressures faced by the school, and asking parents to engage in tax-deductible fundraising activities may require conversion to nonprofit status. Yet the school administration remains so fearful of parental involvement that Knuckleborough refuses to distribute class rosters with student home phone numbers — purportedly to protect families' privacy but more probably to prevent parents from communicating with each other or from organizing pressure of any kind against the school. According to the school's principal (appointed by the proprietor), if parents want to work on beautifying the outside of the school, they are welcome to do so, but "it's been made very clear to them that they may *not* come into the classrooms and decide that they want to change the curriculum. That is *our* responsibility, and they understand it." The school's philosophy, the principal added, is "leave them at the gate, we'll educate!"

This insistence is especially striking because Knuckleborough does not proclaim a particular curricular focus. In the lower grades, teachers follow a curriculum set forth in a textbook series, while in the upper grades the school provides no curricular guidelines to teachers. Not surprisingly, one of the complaints we heard from teachers, particularly in the upper grades, concerned too little curricular direction. Parents, however, are quite satisfied with Knuckleborough Private School. Most students remain in the school for their entire nine-year elementary school careers. The school's attractiveness can be attributed in part to a unique service that public schools can't match: an eleven-and-a-half-hour day, which includes pre- and after-school programs designed for working parents. But whatever the reason for Knuckleborough's parental loyalty, we could not imagine families remaining largely at bay in school matters, in either the public or the other private schools in our sample, where parents were affluent and/or highly educated.

Mandating participation at parochial schools

A requirement that parents perform volunteer work as a condition of enrollment was common in the Catholic schools we observed. Parents must either fulfill specific duties during a certain number of hours per month at the school site or otherwise substitute missed volunteer hours with additional financial contributions. But this requirement for participation does not necessarily translate into parental involvement in classrooms or other academic support. Again, we found that whether it did so was primarily a function of its community's socioeconomic characteristics.

St. Barbara's Elementary, a school serving a middle- to lower-middle-income inner-ring suburb, involves parents in instructional as well as fundraising activities. In addition to requiring parents to attend school-wide meetings (or be fined) and to volunteer 25 hours per year for school fundraising activities, clerical assistance, or classroom assistance, St. Barbara's requires each family to purchase an "agenda book," a colorful and attractively illustrated booklet that includes school rules, health tips, and other relevant information. The books also include weekly calendars with space for students to fill in their daily assignments and to record their completion, plus space for parents to sign indicating supervision of homework. Teachers frequently check for parents' signatures, and the principal walks through each classroom each week to inspect each child's agenda book.

St. Barbara's also prescribes parent involvement with a policy of requiring, without exception, all parents of children in grades K-3 to come to the classroom at the end of the school day to meet their children. There is a $1 per minute fine for parents who are late. This policy not only assures that teachers will not be detained at school caring for young children whose parents are tardy, but also structures a situation in which teachers can speak, each day, with any parent whose child the teacher believes would benefit from such a discussion. These contacts also permit teachers to monitor parent participation. For example, St. Barbara's first-grade parents are expected to read to their first-grade children for a minimum of 15 minutes each evening; parents must sign and send to the teacher a "reading card" testifying that they have accomplished this goal. Teachers report that they are careful to verify that these cards have been signed.

Parent volunteerism in the Catholic schools we observed that serve more disadvantaged populations had, in most cases, quite a different character. Involvement in the academic program was a rare way of meeting "mandated participation" requirements — both because parents did not have the skills or confidence to support the educational program and because the school pressed them to fulfill their commitments by engaging in fundraising, not academic, volunteerism. Routine parental involvement in homework and other academic support was more an exception than the rule, a subject of great faculty frustration.

At St. Milton's, a Catholic school in an inner-city African American community, parents are required to volunteer in the school for 30 hours per year. Few parents actually fulfill this requirement, and many utilize the option to make additional financial contributions in lieu of time. In the case of St. Donat's, a school sited in a low-income community of largely Central American immigrants, many parents do not speak English; as the school has no bilingual program or bilingual staff, involving parents meaningfully in the educational program is not a feasible school ambition. In this, as in other low-income private schools, parent volunteerism is mostly restricted to occasional chaperoning of field trips, fundraising, upkeep of school facilities, and performing administrative duties. There is some evidence that parents resent the schools' frequent appeals for volunteerism, fundraising, and demands for support of their children's academic efforts. As one St. Milton's parent put it, "every time you turn around, there's something that needs selling" — candy, raffles, etc.

If parents were resentful of demands for involvement, we found teachers at these schools equally unhappy that parent participation was so limited. Even at St. Barbara's, and certainly at the more lower-income parochial schools we investigated, teachers frequently complained that some parents felt that, having paid tuition, they had done their share, and it was up to the school to make education successful. A teacher at St. Donat's explained that parents, overall, delegate the responsibility for their children's education entirely to the school and are vexed by the periodic appeals for assistance: parents "resent the school because they feel that we should be able to do everything. They shouldn't have to do anything. They're paying us to take care of all these things."

Parental disengagement, according to St. Donat's staff, has direct consequences for educational outcomes. An upper-grade teacher directly attributed the low academic achievement of her students to lack of parental support and involvement in the schooling of their children:

> [Students] could perform much, much better, but there's nobody after school hours to help them. The students see that it's a waste. [You'd hope that] the parents would understand the importance of their role in the education of their kids.

The vice principal at one of the low-income Catholic schools in our sample suggested that the lack of parental involvement in academic matters was a reflection of a more general disposition toward education in a low-income environment:

> I think part of [the parental disengagement in schooling] may be their culture, too. Education is maybe not the very top, top, top priority on their list. They want the children to be obedient, to behave, to be polite, and such. But education is, because of maybe their background, education is not always their top priority.

In several low-income schools we observed, school staff and parents point fingers at each other to explain why academic achievement is unsatisfactory. Oftentimes, they hold each other responsible for disappointing results; school leaders complain that, without parental support, there is little that they can do to improve academic performance. The following section explores this issue in greater detail.

Begging lower-income parents
to participate in public and private schools

St. Jeremy's Lutheran School serves a lower-middle-class working community.[6] There are few formal requirements for parental involvement beyond paying tuition. One expectation is that, twice a year, parents will per-
sonally come to school to receive their children's report cards from the
teachers. The school makes other efforts to keep parents informed about
academic issues as well. Teachers are expected to send home a weekly
newsletter describing class assignments, and the principal frequently prods
teachers if the newsletter is not produced on time. Some St. Jeremy teachers have policies of requiring parental signatures on homework, although
others do not.

Lay democratic control is a feature of the Lutheran synod to which St.
Jeremy's belongs. Yet because only church members are eligible to serve
on school governing boards, and because few parents are members of the
church, few parents at St. Jeremy's can serve. Thus, as in the more hierarchical Catholic structure, there is no formal mechanism for holding the
school accountable to parents. As an alternative, the school established a
monthly "parent forum," whose meetings any parent can attend. The school
hopes that parents will provide input about policy and become more informed about academic and other school policies. School administrators
and teachers, however, are frustrated that they cannot induce significant
numbers of parents to attend these meetings.

Frustration about inadequate parental participation at such meetings
also characterized school officials at Madison Charter School, a public school
of mostly poor immigrant Latino children. The school was converted to
charter status not in response to parental pressure but rather by a local school
district hoping to boost Madison's very low mean achievement scores (in
the bottom quartile on standardized tests). In fact, the conversion took place
over the initial objections of most Latino parents, who suspected that the
charter might "take away" their community public school. The theory behind the charter, however, was that academic performance would improve
if the school were more accountable to parents.

Parents make up half of Madison's board of directors, and the school,
like St. Barbara's, St. Donat's, St. Milton's, and other private or quasi-public schools we studied, requires parents to make a monthly volunteer commitment. Parents can fulfill this obligation by helping in classes, performing clerical or custodial work, attending governing board or school-wide
meetings (the most common form of participation), or taking English language classes themselves. The school's "parent contract" also requires par-

ents to send children to school on time, observe the school uniform policy, and to check student work folders once a week. Madison has a full-time staff member assigned to helping parents fulfill their four-hour monthly commitment, but, despite these efforts, parental participation has increased only moderately, and the faculty believes that the level of parental support remains insufficient. Goals for test score improvement have not been met, and test results are barely higher than the low pre-charter level that provoked conversion to charter status in the first place. Despite these efforts to *involve* parents, the school cannot be said to be *accountable* to parents in any meaningful sense — the desire for both parental involvement and accountability comes primarily from the school and district professional staff, not from parents themselves.

The levels of parental participation among lower-income public and private schools varied to some extent. Some were more successful than others in getting parents to increase their involvement, minimal though that increase may have been when compared to the standards of the more affluent schools. Yet others that apparently put as much effort into parent recruitment were not so fortunate. One teacher at St. Donat's, for instance, told us that she rarely hears from parents, and "when I do, the parents I do hear from, their child is doing okay. And the ones I don't hear from, those are the ones who are harder to get in touch with....I find that the child who has the most problems, their parents usually are not involved."

St. Felipe's and St. Milton's are located in the same inner-city African American community. Teachers and principals who had taught in both schools reported a dramatic difference in the role of parents in each establishment. In the former, parents were more involved, but too often in a defensive mode to protect their own sons or daughters from academic or behavioral discipline; in the latter, parents left instruction in the hands of the school, to the frustration of teachers wanting parents to be more "involved."

Cultural differences between the ethnic groups in each school may account for some variability in how parents relate to the school. At St. Felipe's, where parents tend to be more involved in school activities, parents are also more suspicious of the religious school faculty and more defensive about faculty judgments regarding their children's academic work or about disciplinary decisions. These parents, African Americans whose origins were in the Southeastern United States, require considerable attention from faculty members, who frequently feel obligated to reassure them of the school's good intentions. The principal has often been successful in this endeavor, and has sometimes been able to recruit parents for a joint effort to improve students' academic performance or behavior. St. Milton's, where parents are less suspicious of school personnel's motives and more willing to defer to teacher and administrator judgments, enrolls students many of whose families are recent immigrants from Belize or, among the African Americans, have origins in French-speaking Louisiana.

Our observations at Mashita Middle School, a predominantly working class public school in our sample, showed that parental unwillingness to defer to school disciplinary decisions is a more widespread problem in contemporary schools, private and public alike. The Mashita principal noted that an increasing share of her time and attention is devoted to handling complaints from parents who question disciplinary decisions of teachers or administrators. This is similar to problems we found at St. Felipe's, St. Donat's, and St. Barbara's, where faculties described an increased willingness of parents to defend their children's misbehavior and to challenge disciplinary actions.

The Mashita principal described the dilemma in the following way. Her words can as easily describe the problems at other schools we observed:

> I think it's critical to have parent involvement but...we've almost...gone too far...when we think that parents can challenge every decision that we make....We are questioned all of the time in a fashion that I don't see as productive. When, for example, I make a decision and a child's parents challenge me...and I...give them a very good explanation of why it was done...they want it their way. So the first thing they...do is call my supervisor, and maybe my supervisor's supervisor....That kind of thing is counter-productive. We've spent way too much emotion and energy in dealing with...over-permissiveness...and we need to be able, in the public schools, to say, "This is not right, we have these rules....Yes, it's a public school and we want you here, but when you do that, you can't be part of the school situation."

Parental opposition to disciplinary decisions at Mashita are exacerbated by the fact that different teachers have different standards; behavior that one teacher might allow, another will not. But while such disparity was apparent in both public and in private schools, the range of disciplinary atmospheres was naturally much greater in a school of 1,700 like Mashita Middle than in a small school of less than 300 like St. Felipe's.

Despite the frustration of having parents challenge disciplinary decisions, the Mashita Middle School principal reported that faculty professional judgment on curricular or instructional issues is almost never challenged by parents, unlike at schools like Olympic Charter, Tatuna Point, or Shalom Ieladim. At Mashita the opposite problem — too much parental passivity — prevails. The Mashita principal and faculty members whom we interviewed complained that their instructional effectiveness was limited by the failure of parents to be involved. In a poll of Mashita faculty, lack of parental support and involvement in the academic program was named the school's most serious problem. The faculty referred to inadequate parent involvement in supervising homework, setting standards regarding the importance of academic work, and communicating to their children that school is important and that children should come to school prepared.

In both public and private schools located in lower-income and lower-middle-class communities, we found teachers making strong efforts to increase parental involvement, often to little avail. One Mashita teacher reports that she devotes one conference period a week to telephoning an equal number of parents whose children are doing well and whose children are not doing well, but gets little constructive response. (Compare this public school teacher's experience with that of the Tatuna Point teacher who receives detailed curricular suggestions from each parent each week.) Parents, the Mashita teacher stated, are not concerned if a child is getting a "D" because they consider this a passing grade. Some parents, on the other hand, reportedly become hostile if the teacher reports a student is not doing well, and they blame the teacher for the child's performance.

Another Mashita teacher described programming the school's automatic computer phone dialer with a message going to at least 10 students' homes each month. The message said, "This is Mrs. VL calling from Mashita Middle School. I just wanted to let you know that I'm having problems with your eighth-grade student....If you would like to know more, please call me." The teacher complained that she had received only one phone call in response, all year, although students did tell her the next day that they got "in trouble." (The teacher also programs a positive message to parents of students who excel, but these are not designed to elicit a return call.) The same teacher noted that she often gets complaints from parents about grades, and even requests for conferences after low grades are issued, but she rues the fact that parents never question the substantive content of her teaching, only the grade.

As part of its Annenberg restructuring,[7] the Mashita Middle School established a "focus group" of parents and teachers to develop ways to increase parent involvement of the supportive type that teachers consider important. The group developed plans for parent training, but there was almost no parental response and the group disbanded.

While lack of parent involvement was a commonly voiced complaint at Mashita Middle School, the issue was rarely raised by the faculty of a demographically similar public school, Ayacucho Elementary School. The difference, however, is not attributable to the greater involvement of Ayacucho parents. Instead, it seems that the Ayacucho faculty assumes that an expectation of significant academic involvement is unrealistic given that many of the school's low-income Latino immigrant parents have had less formal education than their elementary school children. Most Latino parents at Ayacucho say that they are generally satisfied with the school's academic outcomes, in contrast to a small minority of parents and some faculty members who are distressed about low test scores and who voice complaints about the school's lack of consistent high standards. Parents' expectations are frequently limited to a hope that the school will be successful in motivating their children to continue their education — a motivation that, in middle-class communities, schools can assume children bring from home. The school has an expectation that parents will meet twice a year with their child's teacher — once at the beginning of the year to establish goals and once at the end to assess progress — but teachers are convinced that almost any academic progress made by the children will result from the teachers' efforts alone.

Whether this conviction is correct has become an important issue at Renaissance Middle School, a low-income public school that was "reconstituted" by its large urban school district because of a pattern of low test scores. The new principal hired an almost entirely new staff, based on candidates' dedication to the conviction that "all students can learn," yet the new staff has experienced high turnover since reconstitution. One reason for teacher burnout may be the administration's and teachers' efforts to improve academic outcomes without parental support. One teacher explained that, in a normal school, a good teacher will try to meet a student "halfway," with the student's half being the motivation and support he or she brings from home. At Renaissance, the teacher said, teachers attempt to go "90 percent of the way." An expectation that teachers can still succeed in boosting test scores under these circumstances leads to teachers' abandonment of the school in frustration.

This frustration among Renaissance teachers is similar to that of teachers at private St. Milton's and St. Donat's. A Renaissance instructor complained that parents expect teachers to reform behavior that results from a lack of discipline at home; the parents treat the school as a "babysitting center" where they can drop children off in the morning and pick them up in the afternoon or evening without being concerned about what happens in between.

Another low-income public school we investigated has been more effective in encouraging parental involvement and participation in the aca-

demic program. Multicultural Urban Public School is a Title I school operating under a desegregation order. One-third of the student body is Chinese, one-third Latino, one-sixth white, and the balance other minorities.
About 40% of the parents participate on a regular basis — not only in supplementary fundraising activities and attendance at school-wide meetings but
also in classroom work, attendance at parenting classes, and participation
in academic events like "math night."

Three unique features of the school probably contribute to its high
degree of parental participation. First, the school has a balanced ethnic mix
and a vigorous commitment to multilingualism. Not only are limited-En-
glish-proficient students taught in bilingual classes,[8] but PTA meetings are
conducted in English, Spanish, and Chinese, and the school hires parent
coordinators for each of these language groups. Second, family social services — including financial, legal, health, and immigration services — are
coordinated and delivered from the school site. A neighborhood community center works collaboratively with the school to provide parenting classes,
adult literacy classes, and child care. Thus, the school has become not only
an academic institution but a neighborhood service center as well. Third,
the high degree of parental participation may also result from Multicultural
Urban's conscious effort to involve parents in their child's program. Teachers attempt to create homework assignments that involve the child's entire
family. If a child is having either academic or behavioral difficulty, the
school assembles a "school study team" in which the academic staff, school
nurse, and other social service providers join with the child's parents to
review the student's strengths and weaknesses and make recommendations
for home behavioral changes; the team may also put parents in contact with
other service agencies. Through this process, school staff members attempt
to get parents to become mutually responsible for the student's improvement.

A poll of parents several years ago determined that parents wanted
Multicultural to state its mission as preparing every child for college. Not
all teachers were quick to embrace the "college-bound" vision for all students, but the principal recounted that, when there was resistance to this
goal, she "asked [the teachers] what they aspired for their own children." In
the end, the school adopted the college-bound mission.

Yet, this parental involvement in the school's nominal goal has not
translated into specific guidance about practice. At Multicultural, the high
degree of parental involvement is not the same as accountability to parents.
At a meeting of a focus group of parents we assembled for this case study,
not one parent reported ever having a policy disagreement with any faculty
member at the school. This lack of conflict may be the result of a perfect

alignment of parent and faculty goals, but it may also be the case that parents do not feel qualified to evaluate curricular decisions and do not expect to be able to hold the staff accountable in academic decision making. In short, Multicultural has been unusually successful in incorporating parents into its activities and promoting mutual support to enhance student achievement, but parents are largely drawn in by the school, and they act to some extent as its "guests"; they do not operate as independent actors that can hold the school accountable for academic outcomes. Multicultural Urban is but a few miles from Tatuna Point but, in another sense, it is in a different universe.

Our impression that parental demands for accountability and their disposition toward academic involvement vary more by ethnicity and social class than by whether a school is public or private is illustrated by Mashita Middle School's annual "Open House and Parent Conferencing" night. Mashita, as we noted above, is a mostly lower-middle-class or working-class urban school, but it also has a small number of children from a nearby affluent suburban community. One teacher reported that, out of 180 students in her six science classes, only three parents attended Open House. Other teachers we interviewed made similar reports. Parents who participated were mostly from the higher socioeconomic groups, and their children tended to be among the higher achievers. The school has not been successful in bringing into the conferencing events large numbers of parents from relatively lower socioeconomic populations whose children, if they are to succeed in school, may most require their parents' involvement.

At Olympic Charter School, which is more socially, racially, and ethnically integrated than other schools in our sample, parental involvement tends to be structured along race and ethnic lines. The intense parental involvement at Olympic, compared to that at Mashita, may simply reflect the different proportions of parents from the various social classes and ethnic groups. According to a consensus of Olympic faculty and parents whom we interviewed, white (and especially Jewish) parents tend to be more involved than other groups in the school's governing board and in the curriculum and administrative committees; Korean parents tend to volunteer to a greater extent in classrooms, accompany classes on field trips, bring refreshments to classrooms, and participate in fundraising; African American parents attend Governing Board meetings and are active in fundraising, but do not participate much in committee work and tend not to be involved in classrooms; Hispanic parents volunteer little and tend to be involved mostly only if the principal calls them for a specific activity — perhaps because fathers often work evening shifts and mothers stay home with other children.

Mashita Middle School illustrates the complexities of parent involvement in another way. The school is located in a predominantly working-class urban community that borders on an affluent suburb. As we describe further in Chapter 6, the school district established a nearby math and science magnet school as part of a plan to help keep middle-class white families from fleeing the district. The principal of Mashita considers one of her chief problems the fact that, as the most educationally motivated middle-class families in the community choose to send their children to the magnet school, Mashita is losing the parents who were previously a force for higher standards and teacher accountability and were most likely to volunteer and provide additional resources. The principal estimates that the establishment of the magnet school reduced the population of white (and middle-class) families at Mashita from 25% to 19%.

Overall, our observations suggest a pattern in which high-income parents tend to be more involved than are low- and lower-middle-income parents in a variety of school activities and also more at ease in challenging schools with regard to educational practices. At Mashita Middle School, for example, most working parents cannot volunteer in the school for eight hours per month (as Adams Charter School, for example, requires) during the regular school day, and, even if they could, few have the academic skills necessary to assist in a significant way in a middle school educational program. Teachers and administrators at low- and lower-middle-income schools, however, believe that parental disengagement is highly detrimental to student achievement; hence, they attempt to stimulate parental participation in a variety of ways. Many private and charter schools have made parental volunteerism a condition for admission. Under present laws, this option is not viable for neighborhood public schools, regardless of how much the faculty wishes it were otherwise. Nor is it apparent, even if such a condition could legally be imposed, how it could be enforced.

In the cases of lower-income private and charter schools with mandated participation, the terms "parental involvement" and "accountability" have quite different meanings. Parental presence in school affairs remains largely organized and regulated by the school professional staff; it usually does not originate from parents themselves. These schools, in fact, are not accountable to parents; rather, they attempt in a sense to make parents accountable to the school.

In lower-income settings, "accountability" usually resonates more loudly in nonacademic arenas: parents are more likely to hold schools responsible for their children's behavior or safety. As teachers told us in schools like St. Milton's, St. Donat's, or Mashita, parents often refuse to take the blame for their children's misbehavior, yet they also reproach teachers for the school's inability to discipline other parents' children. In general, parents hold these schools most accountable when it comes to safety matters. At Ayacucho Elementary School, for example, the parents, who are mostly uninvolved in academics, were concerned about the potential danger of students running into a nearby highway and successfully demanded that the school build a fence.

Cases of formal accountability to parents

In addition to the presence of parental representatives on school boards of directors at private and charter schools, several schools in our investigation (Shalom Ieladim Jewish School, public Tatuna Point, and Olympic Charter) utilized formal parent accountability systems. These consisted of an annual form sent to parents, which they used to evaluate the school, teachers, administration, and curriculum. At Olympic Charter, receipt of the returned questionnaires is the occasion for a weekend retreat, where the faculty considers what changes might be suggested by the parents' responses. In several cases, teachers reported that they made changes in curricular emphasis based on this feedback. Evaluations were once returned anonymously, but teachers rebelled at the practice, a reflection of their developing frustration about what they regarded as excessive parental interference. Consequently, the system was revised so that all parent evaluations must be signed.

The California archdiocese in which three of the four Catholic schools in our study were located initiated a formal parent feedback system in the year prior to our case studies. Summaries of responses to the questionnaires, which covered school practices and staff, were sent to school principals. Perhaps because the system was new, or perhaps because parents are not as aggressive about making suggestions as they are at Olympic Charter, we did not detect evidence that, at least in the first year, these summaries occasioned any reconsideration of any school policies at the Catholic schools we studied, or that school faculty members considered the exercise particularly worthwhile. The summaries, at least in the schools we studied, reflected general satisfaction with most aspects of the schools.

The limits of accountability to parents in private schools are illustrated by two Catholic schools in our sample, both of which recently disbanded parent advisory councils because parents became too aggressive in proposing policy changes to the school leadership. At St. Felipe's, a group of parents on the school advisory council became excessively (in the principal's view) critical of one of the teachers, and so the principal and pastor disbanded the advisory board. At St. Barbara's, leaders of the parent council thought that discipline was too lax at the school, that basics (like phonics) were insufficiently emphasized in instruction, and that the school did not assign enough homework. (In reality, St. Barbara's was considerably more disciplined, oriented to "basics," and homework-focused than many of the other public and private schools in this sample.) After much argument with parents, the principal and pastor disbanded the council and told the parents that they were free to take their children elsewhere if they did not approve of how the school was run.

Accountability to parents: some observations

Based on our limited sample of eight public and eight private elementary schools, the expectation that private schools are more accountable to parents seems to be untrue. No school could be more accountable to parents for outcomes and practice than Tatuna Point Elementary, a public school in an affluent middle-class suburban community.

We found that in more affluent communities, the patterns of parent accountability in both public and private schools were similar. And in these schools, we also found reason to question the conventional view that making schools more accountable to parents is a certain road to school improvement. The faculties of these public and private schools spend much of their time and energy resisting efforts by parents to hold them accountable for — to meddle in, the faculties would say — professional decision-making in which parents, no matter how well educated, may have a limited perspective.

While this faculty viewpoint may not always appear correct to outside observers, it certainly raises important policy issues about whether a school's accountability to parents is an unalloyed benefit. Our observations led us to conclude that some diminution of parental influence in schools like Tatuna Point or Olympic Charter might be beneficial.

The opposite case is the Liniers French School, where the French government's uniform curriculum policy sharply reduces parents' capacity to demand changes in the school's curriculum and academic practices. And we saw one other private school, Knuckleborough, that felt free to deter parents from interfering in the academic program, both because its middle-class parents had less desire to do so than did the affluent parents at Tatuna Point, and because the school provided a service — before- and after-school care — that was a more important reason for enrollment than the school's academic program. That the two schools in our study (Liniers French and

Knuckleborough) that flatly discouraged parental involvement in the academic program were private schools also contradicts the initial generalization.

To a lesser degree, we observed similar patterns at Shalom Ieladim Jewish School and several Catholic schools. As the principal at Shalom Ieladim told us,

> The position of this school is that parents and the school are not on equal footing. [Shalom Ieladim] has a right to set its own rules and guidelines....There is no shared decision making. Parents put their money and have a say in what goes on, but the ultimate decision is of the school.

As private institutions, private schools have the capacity to shield teachers and administrators from parental demands. School decisions are school prerogatives. It is not the place of parents to set educational policy. Their obligation is to backstop the efforts of the school, not to determine its mission. They do not have ownership over the school; rather, they are primarily consumers of educational services. Ultimately, families are presented with two choices: to accept the school as it is or to find a different institution that better suits their educational expectations. In other words, parents may have the choice to exit private schooling, but they do not necessarily have a voice to shape what occurs there.

Our case studies suggest that parents of public school children can command as much as or more control over educational issues as do parents of private school children — when the parents are affluent, self-confident, and highly educated. But at schools in lower-income communities the pattern is different, with respect to both public and private school parents. Here, parents undertake little effort to make schools accountable for curricular offerings or academic practices; rather, the faculties perceive a serious problem of parental "meddling" in the application of policy to individual children. These faculties experience a mistrust of schools on the part of low-income parents with regard to grades or disciplinary action. Students, of course, no matter what their performance, have always believed that discipline or low grades are "unfair." But faculties at low-income public and private schools report what they believe is a growing tendency on the part of some parents to take the child's viewpoint, minimizing the judgments of school professionals.

Perhaps this sort of advocacy for children on the part of parents is a good thing. In some cases, school principals and teachers reported being able to take this unwanted intervention on the part of parents and turn it to advantage — if they can persuade parents that an initial defense of children's "rights" is ill-advised, and then recruit these parents to more joint responsibility for academic and behavioral outcomes. But, at the very least, these accounts should give pause to uncritical advocacy of greater accountability of schools to parents.

When school reformers talk about schools becoming accountable to parents, another issue often gets confused with accountability. That issue is parent participation, where parents do not attempt to affect school policy but rather take greater responsibility for children's academic and behavioral outcomes in terms defined by school professionals. This kind of participation is akin to making parents accountable to the schools, rather than the other way around.

Developing this kind of parental involvement in a child's success was a major focus of school energies in most of the schools we observed in lower-income and lower-middle-income communities. At more affluent schools, parental support for children's success seemed to be less of a problem. And again, these patterns were common to both public and private schools. The difference was that private schools, and quasi-public schools of choice in our study, were able to require this participation as a condition of enrollment. Regular public schools, at least under current law, cannot do so.

Yet even the private schools, if parents were disadvantaged, had difficulty enforcing these requirements. Where parents did not have the academic skills (or did not feel they had the skills) to participate in the academic program, they were given nonacademic tasks (most often fundraising) to perform. In some cases, parent work schedules made participation at school impossible, and so private schools often made arrangements for parents to buy the time they could not otherwise contribute.

One lower-income school we studied — Multicultural Urban Public School — was somewhat more successful than others in organizing parental involvement in the educational program, but its success seems rooted in its nonacademic activities. Multicultural Urban has become a community service center, developing parental commitment to the school by delivering a range of health, social, and educational services. The school's multilingual faculty also makes great efforts to integrate the curriculum with the family, in a way that seems to go beyond the efforts we saw at other low-income schools, public and private.

Certainly, it will not be easy for other schools, public or private, to imitate the practices of Multicultural Urban. California policy restricting bilingualism in education will make it more difficult, and the coordination of a range of social and educational services can be expensive. If not yet prevalent, however, such coordination is becoming more common in low-income community public schools.

Can public schools learn to mandate parent participation as private and quasi-public schools attempt to do? To do so would require legal changes, and mandatory requirements for participation might stimulate objections by civil libertarians. In some states, legislatures have required minimal participation as a condition of receiving welfare benefits, but no state has yet required parents to meet with teachers without making this a condition of benefit eligibility.

President Clinton has proposed extending the Family and Medical Leave Act to require firms to permit employees to leave work for the purpose of meeting with schoolteachers or attending other school functions. Passage of this proposal would assist not only public schools but also private schools that attempt to enforce mandatory participation rules yet have difficulty doing so. Neither the current family leave law, nor the Clinton proposal, requires employers to compensate such time, as similar laws in some European nations presently do. While an unpaid provision is a step in the right direction, it will not solve the problems faced by several schools we studied, where taking time off from work to visit school was not only impermissible for parents, but also expensive.

Chapter 2

Clarity of Goals and Expectations

The second generalization we examined was that *private elementary schools' outputs and expectations for students tend to be more clearly defined than are public school outputs and expectations.* We found serious conflicts in several schools about what the outputs and expectations of those schools should be but, as in our assessment of accountability to parents, these confusions were present in both public and private schools. In schools without such conflicts, we also discovered a range of clarity regarding expectations for students. In no case, though, did these divisions fall neatly into groups of public vs. private schools. Our observations here again reveal several themes.

Educational policy makers often posit that schools organize themselves around academic achievement objectives, and that private schools are more successful at this. Our research suggests that, in fact, this may not be the case. Schools may organize around a variety of principles different from academic outcomes, such as religious beliefs, safety, or discipline. We observed public schools as successful as private ones in aligning themselves with academic goals, and private schools that hold other values above academic achievement. Moreover, school actors — principals, teachers, parents — in private schools, as well as public ones, may not agree with each other about how objectives should be prioritized. This lack of agreement can result in confusion about whether the schools' primary goal is deepening religious faith, transmitting academic skills, or developing disciplined and moral life habits. At the least, our study suggests that research comparing nonprofit public and private education, and even variation within each sector, has to pay more attention to the array of goals that schools pursue and that parents want them to pursue. Without specifying these goals more clearly, it is difficult to identify whether a school is meeting parent expectations.

The religious character of parochial schools

Not unexpectedly, religious objectives are a central and defining mission of parochial schools. St. Felipe's Elementary School is a case in point. According to the Parent-Student Handbook, "as a Faith Community, the primary purpose of St. Felipe's School is to lead our students to know, to love, to experience Jesus Christ and to spread His saving message throughout the world...." The handbook lists the objectives of the school as being, first, religious; next, moral; next, academic; and finally physical, social, and cultural. The handbook goes on to list parent responsibilities as, first, to "support the teaching of Catholic doctrine, values, traditions, and liturgical practices." Next is to "support the life of the Church through involvement in the...parish." Supporting the policies of the school is next, followed by meeting financial obligations and participating in parent meetings. The seventh in this list of goals is, "as partners in education, support the learning process by establishing a regular time for homework, monitoring television viewing, and assuring that children receive proper rest, exercise and nutrition." The last goal is, "be well informed regarding academic progress."

St. Milton's handbook is similar. It begins by stating that the "distinctive purpose of St. Milton's Catholic School is to proclaim the gospel message of Jesus Christ," and it then lists the school's objectives, with purely academic outcomes far down on the list. These schools' leadership teams are consistent in reflecting this philosophy. St. Milton's principal states that, if religion is properly taught, academic outcomes will take care of themselves: "The academics flow from that [religious instruction], but our first and foremost reason for being here is the moral education of the children."

Asked to describe the mission of the school, St. Felipe's pastor stated that it was to "provide...ways in which people can grow their faith,...to grow as followers of Christ,...to make sure the children have been taught a rich education, that children who want to are helped to grow in the Catholic faith, [and,] if you're not Catholic, that they give opportunities to learn what the Catholic is so they can become Catholic. And to provide liturgies for the children." The school's principal adds that, although many children at the school are Baptists, "if you are non-Catholic and you attend our school, you must take Catholic religion."

We found parents willing to make great concessions to these private schools' defined missions. The Catholic schools, for example, make catechism a compulsory subject within their curricula. Although in some of these schools non-Catholic students may be a large proportion of the student body, parents agree to have their children partake daily in a 45-minute religious course, as well as in many other religious activities, without exception. This may amount to approximately 15-20% of the total time that students spend in school.

In some cases we observed directly how scholastic and religious goals may come into conflict. At St. Barbara's, there was an ongoing dispute between the parish pastor and the school principal about whether the school's mission was primarily pastoral or academic. Because the school had nearly twice the number of applicants as seats, admission choices frequently had to be made between, on the one hand, students who scored low on academic tests but were children of parishioners and, on the other, students from outside the parish whose academic scores were higher. Oftentimes, the pastor deferred to the principal's wish to create a school with a strong academic reputation; but just as frequently, the principal was pressured to make exceptions in her admissions policy in favor of parish children who tested poorly. In some cases, applicants rejected on the basis of low test scores were told they could re-apply if, after a year in the local public school, their test scores had improved. The pastor of St. Barbara's insisted to us that "we're not a successful school if our students get into Harvard but in the process drop the Catholic Church. The principal reason for the school is to hand down the Catholic faith."

At the low-income St. Milton's and St. Felipe's schools, of course, admission to a metaphorical Harvard was not even contemplated as an ambition. And at St. Barbara's, even the principal does not hold an exclusively academic view of school goals, but represents a middle ground. If she emphasizes the academic side of the school more than does the pastor, many teachers and parents emphasize academics more than does the principal. Several teachers we interviewed objected, for example, to time taken from academic pursuits for religious instruction, participation in Mass and other religious ceremonies, and school social-religious activities. Parents also sometimes complained to the school that too much time was taken away from academic pursuits by the religious activities in which students participate. Some parents we interviewed sent their children to St. Barbara's primarily because they believed that a Catholic school provides superior instruction (which they may have defined as "traditional" instruction, like emphasis on phonics), or because they believed it will prepare their children to compete for admission to regional academic Catholic high schools, where passing an academic admission test is the gateway. These parents considered St. Barbara's strong religious component a distraction from the school's primary mission.

In both low- and middle-income private religious schools, another theme emerged repeatedly. Regardless of whether the school staff saw the school's mission as primarily academic or primarily religious, parents were attracted by neither of these goals: they sent their children to these schools mostly because they believed them to be safer than public schools. Whether these parents' perceptions of the relative safety of neighborhood public schools was accurate,[9] the parents were relatively indifferent to the school's expectations, regardless of how clearly stated, so long as the school environment was free of violence.

Despite these schools' very clear description of their missions, desire for exposure to Catholicism was not the motivating factor behind most parents' decisions to send their children to St. Felipe's or St. Milton's, although it was indeed the case for some. Most of these schools' families sent their children because they believed the schools were safe or had a reputation for strict discipline.

We found a similar situation at St. Donat's, a low-income Catholic school whose families, unlike those of St. Felipe's and St. Milton's, are Central American immigrants, not African Americans. In this case, too, while the school proclaims its mission as being a religious one, the principal acknowledges (and our interviews with parents confirmed) that most families who send their children to St. Donat's do so because they believe it is safer than public schools. While some parents thought that St. Donat's offered a superior academic education, a teacher assessed typical parents of her students this way: "They'll agree to the religion even if they don't necessarily want it that much...because they want their kid in a safe place."

Broader educational goals vs. testable outcomes

In several schools in our sample, some public and some private, we witnessed great tension with respect to the academic focus different educational actors — school staff, parents, district administrators — believed that instructors should follow. While teachers, overall, espoused the importance of pursuing broad curricular and pedagogical goals, some parents or district officials tended to be mostly concerned about testable outcomes. Faculty defenders of broad curricular goals believed that testable outcomes are narrow academic objectives that do not provide a rounded education. In turn, those concerned with standardized test attainment emphasized how these evaluations may affect the reputation of their school or serve as a gateway for educational opportunities for students.

In Chapter 1, we described a conflict between teachers and parents about how standardized tests would affect instruction at Shalom Ieladim Jewish School. Teachers resisted parent demands for a greater emphasis on testable outcomes primarily because they felt the school should aim for other evaluation methods that measured broader abilities and skills; they also feared that the school's expectations for children would shift away from creative or critical thinking competencies if standardized tests were adopted.

Within the public sphere, we saw indications of similar conflict about what a school's outcomes should be at Olympic Charter School. At this school, while some parents supported the faculty's constructivist pedagogical orientation, there were many parents who ignored the school's clear self-definition and posited goals for the school that were measurable by standardized test scores. These latter set of parents wanted a more exclusive focus on academic preparation for college entrance exams (though taking these would be many years' distant for elementary school children). On the other side, the school faculty, along with a very vocal group of parent leaders, openly rejected standardized testing and the skills these tests assessed. Tension between parents and faculty over these different curricular emphases was a constant theme at the school. The school communicated its constructivist philosophy very explicitly to all parents and prospective parents. Nonetheless, many parents did not take this message seriously and sought to impose a more traditional educational program. Perhaps because this urban school attracted a middle-class clientele, parents assumed it would be organized like middle-class suburban schools, where preparation for college entrance exams was an implicit and shared first priority.

It would be difficult to imagine a school where expectations are more openly defined than Olympic. The faculty frequently debates and adjusts the proper balance between basic skills instruction vs. critical thinking skills and individuality. The school announces its adherence to constructivism at every opportunity, and this pedagogy comes packaged with a gestalt of other explicit political and subcultural values. When the school chose a new principal several years ago, one of the central criteria established for candidates by the parent interviewing committee was the principal's willingness to support the teachers' union position in the event of a district-wide teachers' strike. Environmentalism is central to the school's curriculum, but at times the environmental theory being taught goes beyond scientific consensus and blends into fadism — the school's promotional material, for example, states that "children learn about the nutritious value of what they grow [in the school garden]...and discover the differences between food that is grown organically and food that is produced through petrochemical-stimulation."

One parent leader described Olympic's objectives like this: "We end up with loud-mouth kids in a good sense [even if] their math facts aren't memorized as well. You know, they go to junior high school and they say,

'Oh, gee, he doesn't know his twelve times tables like he should,' [but] our kids know how to speak up, ask questions, and give opinions." And one veteran teacher explained why she pays no attention to children's scores on standardized tests: The tests, she complained, have reading test comprehension questions that are "fact-finding, not...'what do you think about it?'" But everything she teaches, she said, "is a 'what-do-you-think-about' or 'do you agree or disagree and why or why not' question....We want our kids to be free little thinkers. And that's more important to us." Nonetheless, despite its lofty goals and clearly stated mission, Olympic Charter found itself having to accommodate and cater to both sets of parents, and ultimately to compromise to some extent the values that its parent leaders, principal, and faculty hold dear.

The story of Olympic Charter repeats itself at Adams Charter Middle School. The disjunction between school curricular goals and parent expectations has become increasingly deeper over time. The school was founded with a thematic emphasis on the arts, but (as described in Chapter 1) not all parents who chose the school did so for this reason. For many, Adams is attractive primarily because of its small size and the safety this size implies. Parents are not as motivated as the staff to deviate from the curriculum offered at the regular district middle schools, and if the regular schools offer eighth-grade algebra, the parents believe that Adams should as well, even if this means less emphasis on artistic and creative activities, presumably the school's *raison d'etre*.

A diffusion of academic expectations also characterizes Ayacucho, a regular neighborhood public school. Here, the conflict is not between faculty and parents, but between faculty and district administration. At Ayacucho, the school faculty had been organized, at least nominally, around raising academic outcomes, and it undertook major reforms in an attempt to raise the low level of academic skills. As part of this effort, the school adopted a coherent "developmental learning" philosophy, including whole language reading instruction, cooperative learning, multi-grade classrooms, and narrative (as opposed to letter-grade) report cards. When these reforms were unsuccessful in raising test scores, Ayacucho's school district intervened and substituted clear district learning standards for each skill and grade level. The faculty is disturbed, wondering why its prior reforms were unsuccessful and unsure if the new standards-based programs will be more so.

In this case, parents are concerned about the school, but, unlike Adams and Olympic parents, they rely on the principal and teachers to discuss and recommend academic changes. Parents seem generally satisfied with the school's academic outputs and expectations, and, like parents at the low-income parochial schools we studied, their primary concern is school safety.

They insisted, as noted above, that the playground should have a fence, and they are concerned about fights between children and inadequate supervision during lunch and before and after school.

Two other public schools — Renaissance Middle School and Multicultural Urban Public School — were very specific about their academic goals and expectations, and their energies were organized around a diverse group of academic, behavioral, and social service programs to support these goals. As clear as "critical thinking" is to the definition of outcomes at Olympic, equally clear is Renaissance's stated commitment to improvement of tested academic skills. The school defines its mission as a series of core beliefs, such as: "All individuals can and want to learn; learning can be subdivided into specific concrete competencies; if individuals do not learn, then those assigned to be their teachers should accept responsibility for this failure and should take appropriate remedial action." Yet despite this explicit focus on learning as the expectation of the school, much of the school's resources and energy go into community outreach, coordination, and provision of family health, mental health, and social work services — even assistance in finding after-school jobs. Each of these programs is justified in terms of the readiness for academic learning it provides. While these programs may have value in themselves, it remains to be seen whether, or to what extent, they will ultimately succeed in their academic objectives, or even whether the school's emphasis on these programs will conflict with the clarity of its academic ambitions. (A similar mix of social service and academic programs seems much more successfully focused on academic outcomes at Multicultural Urban Public School.) As noted earlier, at Renaissance, some teachers find the school's lofty academic expectations to be inconsistent with the disadvantages their students face, and the teachers leave in frustration.

Reconstituted by its district specifically because of low scores on norm-referenced tests, Renaissance Middle School also illustrates that conflict between academic goals, as defined by teachers and schools and by standardized tests, is not unique to a self-consciously "constructivist" school like Olympic. While Renaissance's goal of improving student academic achievement is as explicit and focused as any school we observed, teachers feel that standardized tests interfere with this goal as much as help it. For example, the school's curriculum emphasizes an "inquiry approach" to mathematics (consistent with the National Council of Teachers of Mathematics standards), but the district's California Test of Basic Skills (CTBS) emphasizes computation. Teachers, therefore, report that they have found it necessary to ignore the school's stated curriculum in order to prepare students to score higher on the CTBS.

Like Renaissance, Multicultural Urban, the Title I school with a "whole child" orientation, also operates a combination of social service and academic programs. Some Multicultural faculty members feel that the proper balance between academic and social service goals has not been found, although others believe that integrated social services are an essential precondition for academic progress and that therefore the social and academic goals are indistinguishable.

Nominally, as noted in Chapter 1, Multicultural Urban has had a single theme for the last two years, proclaimed in literature and posted throughout the school: every child will go to college. However, it is too early to determine whether this goal will be realized or to what extent. Without intermediate expectations, the goal is more a symbolic than a practical one that can guide school policy. In the shorter term, teachers at Multicultural Urban were unhappy about their district's emphasis on standardized testing, which they viewed as forcing them to emphasize narrow testable skills to the exclusion of other equally important academic goals.

In California, as elsewhere in the nation, there has been increased emphasis in recent years on accountability for defined academic standards. The school district in which both Mashita Middle School and Olympic Charter School are located has adopted a set of learning standards for each subject and grade level, and these standards are posted throughout Mashita Middle School on large colorful posters. Expectations, therefore, are nothing if not clearly defined. The district also recently adopted the Stanford Achievement Test as its assessment measure, primarily because it became convinced that this test, as opposed to others previously used, was better aligned with the "higher order thinking" skills that the district learning standards attempt to emphasize. If the curriculum is being followed, district officials believe, children should do well on the Stanford test.

We found some evidence that the district's strategy of aligning standards and assessment in this fashion may be having its desired effect. One Mashita science teacher reported that she had been so impressed with how questions were asked on the test (e.g., asking students to interpret graphs and reason logically from presented information, rather than repeat memorized facts), that she would henceforth attempt to change her teaching to be more consistent with that type of assessment.

But this teacher was an exception rather than the rule. Most Mashita teachers we interviewed considered the district's "learning standards" to be unrealistic for their school because many students, coming from more disadvantaged families, read below the norm for their grade level.[10] Mashita staff members also find Stanford test results especially discouraging because they know that many parents compare Mashita scores to those at other nearby schools whose populations are more affluent. Some teachers have concluded that there is little that can be done in the way of preparation, practice, or curriculum realignment to change this reality. Nonetheless, in the week prior to testing, teachers reluctantly administered practice tests from booklets furnished by Harcourt-Brace, the test publisher.

In this respect, the feelings of teachers at lower-income public schools like Multicultural Urban, Renaissance, or Mashita parallel those of teachers at more privileged private schools like Shalom Ieladim or at less conventional quasi-public schools like Olympic. In each case, teachers feel that imposition of standardized testing interferes with their efforts to define a unique set of academic expectations for their students, expectations that are either appropriate to their students' disadvantages or that are more aligned with pedagogies emphasizing more difficult-to-test skills — or both.

Anchoring expectations in scripture: a school falls apart

One of the private religious schools we studied experienced such an extreme schism over the definition of behavioral expectations for students that it closed at the end of the year in which the case study was conducted. St. Jeremy's Lutheran School was organized democratically, consistent with Lutheran Church-Missouri Synod principles. Ultimate authority for the school rested in the parish's Voters' Assembly, which in turn elected a school board who hired the principal and oversaw all school policies. During the year in which we visited the school, the principal and his faculty attempted to impose a strict "assertive discipline" program, in which rewards and punishments were predictably meted out for compliance or noncompliance with school rules. The program culminated in a "three strikes, you're out" policy, in which points accumulated from three infractions (they could be as minor as not having a uniform shirt tucked in) led to automatic suspension.

The church pastor and school board had a more relaxed attitude toward student misbehavior, and frequently overturned suspensions and milder disciplinary decisions taken by the faculty. The dispute that erupted consumed the school for an entire year and was couched in scriptural terms (the pastor's editorial in the church newsletter, for example, was headlined "'Assertive Discipline' is All Law and No Gospel"; a written response by the faculty stated that "no chastening seems to be joyful for the present, but grievous; nevertheless, afterward it yields the peaceable fruit of righteousness to those who have been trained by it," and it accused the board of failing to act "according to Matthew 18" and of violating the eighth commandment.) The church membership was divided between traditionalist disciplinarians and progressives; parents were mostly divided between those whose children did not run afoul of the rules and those whose children did — the latter group found it could successfully appeal to the school board to get the principal's disciplinary decisions overturned. Because there was no higher church body or school district with authority over the school, there was no way to resolve this dispute. And during the entire final year, arguments about disciplinary policy eclipsed discussions about academic or other goals the school might have had.

We have the impression that, were it not for the controversy over disciplinary policy, we would have observed the same confusion over goals at St. Jeremy's that we observed at comparable Catholic schools: clearly defined school expectations about the primacy of religious outcomes, with most (though not all) parents ignoring these and sending their children to the school because it was perceived to be either safer or more traditionally disciplined than the local public school. In our interviews, however, concern about the disciplinary controversy crowded out reflections about other school goals or their relative priorities. We had two hints, however, that academic goals were not the top priority for those responsible for the school's operation.

First, while the Stanford Achievement Test had been administered annually for many years, it was not until this last year that the St. Jeremy School Board (which at this time was at odds with the principal over disciplinary matters) asked to see reports of test scores. Second, several years prior to our case study, St. Jeremy's lost its accreditation from the Western Association of Schools and Colleges. No parent with whom we spoke raised this as a concern, and the principal told us that perhaps the following year the school might begin the self-study process required to obtain new accreditation. Contrast this casual attitude with that of more affluent parents at the Shalom Ieladim Jewish School, who insisted, over the objections of the school faculty, that the school seek accreditation.

Clarity of goals: some observations

In many of the schools in our study, we found not so much a lack of clarity about goals and expectations but rather a multitude of goals on the part of important actors.

Disagreement about goals was especially striking in the low-income Catholic schools we studied. There, the explicit religious mission seemed to be at variance with the ambitions and expectations of many parents who send their children to these schools. Placed in historical perspective, these schools' own definition of their mission is unsurprising. Separate systems of Catholic schools were established in America's cities not to provide a safer environment than the public schools or to do a better job of teaching reading or arithmetic, but rather to teach religious faith to Catholic children and to make that teaching central to the school experience. As New York City's Catholic Church announced in 1840, "Religion forms a vital part of education" (Ravitch 1974, p. 44).

This truth, however, has sometimes been lost in today's public debates, whether regarding philanthropic plans to fund scholarships for poor non-Catholic children to attend Catholic schools, or in legal battles regarding whether tax-supported dollars can properly fund educational vouchers for Catholic schools. Scholarly debates attempt to measure the reading and arithmetic scores that result from trials of these plans, but if our observations are typical, these debates miss an important point. If Catholic schools are effective in teaching reading and arithmetic, this is still only a secondary priority.[11] These case studies cause us to wonder if parents recruited to utilize these scholarships and vouchers are always fully aware of the fundamental purposes of the schools to which they send their children.

A similar conflict was illustrated most starkly in our investigation of St. Jeremy's Lutheran School. Here, the faculty and lay board were consumed by a policy debate grounded in Lutheran scriptural interpretation, while barely any children attending the school were of the Lutheran faith. Few, if any, parents who sent their children to St. Jeremy's did so with expectations for outcomes that were aligned with those of school leaders.

At several public schools and some elite private schools in our sample, we found less dramatic disputes over goals. If our case studies are typical, however, the growing focus of educational policy makers on aligning curricula with standardized tests is creating in some cases a potentially serious split with teachers, who remain unpersuaded that these tests measure the outcomes the tests aim to produce. We found such splits emerging at both elite private schools and at public schools of choice. In some of these, faculties defined academic success differently than did either policy makers or many parents. In public schools in lower-income communities, we found similar concerns; in addition, teachers at these schools worried that standardized tests suggested inappropriate comparisons with schools in more affluent communities. They also wondered about how academic achievement of any kind should rank in priority with other nonacademic health and social services.

Testable outcomes are often advanced by policy makers as an important signal by which parents making school selections can assess the relative educational quality of schools. Our research suggests that this may not be true of all parents. Our interviews and observations suggest that families that attend public and private schools in high-income neighborhoods tend to pay close attention to standardized test results and do in fact desire to compare how different schools score on these measures. On the other hand, families that attend public and private schools in low-income neighbor-hoods seem to be largely oblivious to standardized tests — parents do not seem to be attuned to test scores and do not appear to use them as a gauge to compare their schools to other institutions. Instead, in these schools, the primary concern of parents we interviewed was school safety — insisting that the playground have a fence, that fights between children be prevented, and that lunchtime and before- and after-school activities be adequately supervised.

Chapter 3

Behavioral and Value Objectives

The third generalization we examined was that *private elementary schools tend to produce higher nonachievement outputs — behavior and values, for example — than do public elementary schools, and private schools allocate a higher proportion of resources to these nonacademic objectives than do public schools.* Here we found schools in our limited sample where behavioral and value objectives were more important, relative to academic goals, than in other schools, but, with respect to this measure, schools again did not divide neatly along public vs. private lines.

Of course, as Chapter 2 makes clear, this generalization was by definition true for the private religious schools we studied. Religion and/or cultural studies were central parts of the curriculum at the Shalom Ieladim Jewish School, at the four Catholic elementary schools in our sample, and at St. Jeremy's Lutheran School. At Shalom Ieladim, about 30% of the school day — more around Jewish holidays — is devoted to Hebraic and Jewish studies. Catechism, attendance at Mass, and other religious instruction consumed an important part of the school day at the Catholic and Lutheran schools as well.

Teaching the ethical values that are central to these religious traditions was also an important priority at the Jewish and Catholic schools we studied. Recall from Chapter 2 that the St. Felipe's handbook listed moral objectives ahead of academic ones; the practices we observed at schools like this confirmed this priority. These schools make canned food drives for the homeless, visits to convalescent homes, and a host of similar social service activities an important part of their daily curricula.[12]

Only at the Shalom Ieladim Jewish School, and at the predominantly Latino Catholic schools in our sample — St. Barbara's and St. Donat's — did all, or nearly all, of the students share the faith or culture of the school. At St. Jeremy's Lutheran School virtually none of the students were Lutheran, and at the Catholic schools located in African American inner-city communities, students were as likely to be Baptist as Catholic. We have no evidence of the extent to which these schools were successful in reinforcing the religious values of the students, or in converting students to the schools' faiths, although these nonacademic objectives were paramount in the schools' missions. This finding reinforces the notion that parents do not necessarily espouse the primary nonacademic objectives of religious schools. Only in the Shalom Ieladim Jewish School can we attest that religious instruction was a key factor that prompted parents to select this particular establishment for the education of their children. In fact, the school's admission policy explicitly favors applicants for whom the religious, and not the academic, aspect is a primary motivation. As the president of the board suggests, "there are many excellent public schools in this area" for families whose goals are primarily academic.

With regard to other (than religious) values and behavioral objectives, we found examples of emphases on these in both public and private schools. Certainly in some of the Catholic schools we observed, the disciplinary atmosphere was more orderly and "traditional." At St. Barbara's, for example, it was difficult for us to conduct unobtrusive classroom observations because, at the moment an author of these case studies entered a classroom, students stood and said "good morning" in unison. Yet behavioral objectives were also important at public schools. At Ayacucho Elementary School, the entire faculty has coordinated its teaching of "megaskills," such as respect and cooperation. Every classroom has these listed on the wall and every teacher stresses them. At Mashita, a uniform dress policy was adopted several years ago, and teachers report that discipline has improved significantly as a result.

At Multicultural, despite its ambitious theme of "every child will go to college," there was little clarity about intermediate academic goals. There was significantly more clarity, however, about immediate behavioral objectives, considered as important as the academic. The school has adopted a packaged conflict-management program ("TRIBES") that is organized around four behavioral norms: attentive listening, mutual respect, no put-downs, and the "right to pass" (i.e., the right not to answer a personal question during a standard TRIBES group activity). Each teacher displays the norms in his or her classroom, in whatever languages are appropriate. The program includes a parent training component, and many parents have participated. Fourth-grade leaders are trained as "peer tutors," and fifth-grade leaders are trained as "conflict managers," responsible to intervene in any potential conflicts they see on the playground.

As described in Chapter 2, behavioral objectives are also important at the quasi-public Olympic Charter School. Here the behavioral objectives are a willingness to question authority, both academic and nonacademic.

In one respect, the variety of objectives incorporated into school missions was determined in part by schools' financial resources. Some lower-income private religious schools we observed were able only to offer basic academic and religious instruction and had no resources to deliver extracurricular programs (band, music, sports) that the staff considered necessary to develop the nonacademic values and behaviors essential to an adequate education. Indeed, several parochial school teachers told us that they send their own children to public schools, primarily because of the greater availability of such resources. Because the press often presents anecdotal stories of public school teachers who send their children to private schools, these contrary anecdotes were not stories we expected to hear.

In sum, we observed schools emphasizing behavioral and value objectives in both public and private nonprofit sectors. The most elite of the schools we studied, Liniers French School and Tatuna Point, were also the most single-mindedly academic of the group; the former a private school, the latter public. Shalom Ieladim, also elite and academic, supplemented this focus with a religious emphasis. While the religious schools make nonacademic goals (not only religious practice, but also discipline and the ethical systems that are central to these religious traditions) a high priority, so too do some public schools (like Multicultural and Renaissance) in low-income communities, where conflict management is an important part of the curriculum.

Public schools that fund extracurricular activities like sports, band, and clubs, designed to teach behavioral (teamwork) and leadership skills, apparently have adopted a mission that goes beyond a narrow academic focus. Private schools where these activities are too expensive may have difficulty focusing on these nonacademic behavioral objectives, notwithstanding their commitment to do so. In short, the notion of private schools doing a better job of meeting behavioral objectives, while public schools aim at academic outcomes, if any at all, cannot accurately be applied to all public and private schools, based on the case studies reported here.

Chapter 4

Clear Standards for Teacher Selection and Retention

There seems to be a widely held belief that one of the most important differences between public and private schools is the laxity of teacher standards stimulated by public employee protections and unionization. To address this notion, we considered the generalization that *private schools' teacher selection and retention criteria are more clearly defined than are selection and retention criteria for teachers at public schools.*

Our observations and interviews do not confirm this expectation. With regard to teacher selection, in some of the low- and middle-income private schools (both secular and religious) we studied, salary scales were generally so low, compared to those at public schools, that teacher selection could rarely be based primarily on an assessment of teaching skill or curricular approach. Principals assumed that the most academically skilled teachers would not be available to them. In some cases young, apparently highly skilled teachers obtained their teaching credentials while effectively serving an apprenticeship at Catholic schools, and then applied for positions at public schools because of the pay differentials.

At St. Felipe's, for example, low salaries and poor teaching conditions considered generally undesirable (in a poor African American community) contributed to a 50% annual turnover rate for faculty. In the for-profit Knuckleborough School serving lower-middle- and middle-income students, the original proprietor had an explicit policy of keeping salaries low (in 1997, they averaged about $24,000 a year) and class sizes small. The owner believed that he could offset the teacher quality loss from low salaries, first, by investing heavily in professional development for teachers and, second, by benefiting from the enthusiasm that young first-year teachers — always plentiful because of the high turnover resulting from low salaries — would bring to the job. This enthusiasm, he reasoned, would offset teachers' lack of skill and experience. Regardless of whether this theory had merit, the subsequent (and present) proprietor has maintained low salaries, but without the investment in professional development. The result is a 40% annual turnover rate in the teaching faculty, with newly

48

hired inexperienced teachers never gaining the opportunity at Knuckle–borough to develop into skilled professionals. Teachers usually find placement within the local school district after one or two years of service.

On the other hand, we discovered that schools may be attractive to teachers for other nonmonetary reasons. Teachers at St. Milton's and St. Donat's, for instance, assert that they have opted to teach in an inner-city Catholic school, rather than migrate to a better-paying post at a public school, because of a more attractive working environment than that offered by local public schools. Others suggest a commitment to their school's particular pedagogical approach or spiritual philosophy. Some say that they seek out schools where students come from fairly advantageous backgrounds, while others emphasize their desire to work in underprivileged communities.

We now turn our attention to various factors that shape teachers' selection and retention.

Faculty collegiality

Oftentimes, teachers are attracted to schools where the faculty operates in a tight-knit congenial environment. At St. Barbara's, for instance, an apparently highly qualified local public school teacher was recruited when the principal became impressed with the preparation of first graders who transferred to St. Barbara's from the neighborhood public school. As a result, she aggressively recruited the public school's kindergarten teacher, who accepted the St. Barbara's position despite the cut in pay, because she liked the communal "family" atmosphere she found at the Catholic school.

We found teacher appreciation for such collegiality at several other schools as well. The defining character of these schools was not necessarily their small size, although private schools are more likely to be small. Nor was their defining characteristic public or private organization, although we were somewhat more likely to find such collegiality at small religious private schools. We heard reports of high degrees of faculty cohesion at each of the Catholic schools we studied, at the Lutheran school, at the Jewish school, and at the quasi-public Olympic and Adams charter schools. This was not a characteristic of the 450-student Ayacucho Elementary, nor of the 1,700-student Mashita Middle. Nor did it characterize Renaissance or Tatuna Point schools, each of which enrolled about 500, perhaps because the faculty were under such pressure at these schools for better results, at the former from the administration and at the latter from parents. However, we did find a collegial atmosphere at 700-student Multicultural public school, where the faculty embraced a common challenge to raise the achievement of students.

In our experience, this sense of collegiality was nourished by a variety of factors. In many schools, the principal paid a key role in fostering an environment conducive to reflection, exchange, and personal interaction. In others, the school's mission was to operate as a community center — the children's socioemotional needs were on a par with their academic ones, and this requirement of community necessarily had to include the teaching staff. There were also some schools that espoused a particular pedagogical or academic objective that rallied the staff together. In all these instances, collegiality had a significant impact in the professional performance of teachers and principals; and much of their devotion and commitment to their students found strength and encouragement through the support of their peers.

Hiring standards and teacher quality

When asked what they sought in teacher candidates, public school principals we interviewed were more likely to emphasize pedagogical skill and intellectual qualifications, in addition to personal characteristics, while the private school principals (particularly in low-income religious schools) were more likely to emphasize affective and personal characteristics first and teaching skill secondarily.

For instance, the St. Felipe's principal stated that she is primarily interested in the prospective teacher's family background and religious orientation: "I'm not saying that they have to be Catholic, but I think it's important [if they are going to teach] here, that they...really believe in God." After satisfying herself on this count, she takes the candidate to the classroom for which she is hiring, and asks the candidate to teach a sample lesson. At St. Barbara's, the main component of the principal's new teacher interview are questions about how the teacher would handle hypothetical disciplinary problems in the classroom. Next in importance was the teacher's personal religious practice.

In the case of St. Jeremy's Lutheran School, teachers were almost exclusively recruited from graduates of the Missouri Synod's Concordia teachers' colleges. Each Concordia graduate has an academic major and a religion minor. In the few cases where a teacher was hired who was not a Concordia graduate (for example, in one case the school hired a recent graduate from the local nondenominational Bible college), St. Jeremy's required the teacher to attend Concordia to take courses in religion during her first years of teaching. The principal of St. Jeremy's told us that when he interviews prospective teachers he mostly seeks to explore "their allegiance to the faith, their doctrinal understanding." Inquiries into candidates' pedagogical philosophy were unnecessary, he stated, because the school had adopted a curriculum guide, and teachers needed only to follow it.

The principals of St. Milton's and St. Donat's told us that they do not hire a teacher until they determine that the instructor has good rapport with children. Their primary interest in examining prospective teachers' academic records is to make sure the candidate has taken courses in child development. In these Catholic schools, teacher candidates are likely to be parishioners, parent volunteers who have obtained (or are getting) a college degree, or friends of teachers already on the staff. Thus, the principal is likely to be more familiar with these prospective teachers than would be a principal in a large, more impersonal, public school.

In one of the Catholic schools we studied — St. Felipe's — the principal asked her most senior teacher to interview candidates as well, and then asked for this teacher's advice before making her final decision. This process is even more far-reaching at St. Donat's. There, teacher candidates are asked to spend a full day at the school, mingling with the staff, so that the principal can get evaluations from any teachers who wish to offer advice about the potential candidate.

At Shalom Ieladim, teachers are fully responsible for selecting prospective teachers, and pedagogy is one of their primary selection criteria. As the principal explained,

> I set up a situation in the school where no teacher comes into the school unless all the teachers have seen them teach, have interviewed them, and we agree that this would be an asset to the faculty. So every teacher who comes into this school — all the teachers feel [they] are excellent teachers, as well as I feel that. In fact, what I basically do is I bring maybe three candidates that I think would be excellent for the school. Then we put them through this testing and interview process. So, when I hire a teacher, I feel this is someone who can bring something really good to the school.

The peer selection of staff is also instrumental in creating a tight feeling of community among teachers. An upper-grade teacher reflects that this is imperative in creating a cohesive teacher group "because in the end [the principal] can always say: you chose her. It wasn't me imposing this person upon you. You chose them so let's work with this." Moreover, the current hiring practices impart a sense of security to newcomers. As one newly hired teacher noted, "when the other teachers saw me, they were confident enough in my abilities at that point that I could either learn more or get to a point that I didn't have to feel I had to prove myself."

Olympic Charter, a school that explicitly espouses a constructivist pedagogical philosophy, also uses a peer selection process. Here, a staff committee made up of parents and teachers hires new staff after candidates are interviewed by all teachers and parents who wish to participate. In addition, because all teaching at Olympic is team teaching (classrooms each have two teachers, with as many as 65 students), the potential partner for each candidate is given veto power over the selection.

A teacher shortage in California may be having a serious impact on standards for teacher selection at both public and private schools. Because California chose to implement a class-size reduction in grades K-3 within a two-year period, teacher shortages have spread throughout the public school system. Thus, at Mashita Middle School, while the principal states that she previously placed great emphasis on pedagogical philosophy and skill in selecting teachers, she can no longer do so because she now must select from a pool of uncredentialed teachers who possess insufficient background to be able to answer pedagogical questions. Instead, she evaluates candidates primarily on the basis of interpersonal factors — how well the candidate relates to her and how enthusiastic and self-confident the candidate appears. The principal's view is that teaching requires interpersonal skills, and, while mistakes will be made by evaluating candidates primarily on this basis, there is no alternative when the pool consists almost entirely of those without experience. The principal estimates that, at most, she has dismissed about 20% of the probationary teachers she has hired because they were inadequate to the job. In almost all cases, their inadequacy consisted of an inability to maintain control of their classrooms.

The impact of supply-and-demand factors for teachers is most dramatically illustrated at the Liniers French School. Here, for teachers of the French curriculum, the school receives about 100 applications for each position from French nationals seeking a teaching experience in the United States. The school sifts through the applications, then interviews the finalists and makes its selections in Paris. For American teachers of the English curriculum, however, the Liniers French School faces the same problems as do other private schools in California. Liniers' salaries are considerably less than public school salaries, and so the statewide teacher shortage causes the school to have great difficulty attracting highly qualified applicants.

In sum, while a teacher shortage has affected the ability of both public and private schools to hire desired candidates, some schools maintain clear standards by which they select new faculty. Not surprisingly, the standards are not necessarily uniform across schools, nor do they primarily involve academic preparation or pedagogical skill. Regardless of the expectations that parents may have of these schools, faculties and administrators at establishments with a self-conscious unique pedagogy or a distinctive religious purpose select new teachers primarily in fulfillment of these goals.

Formal teacher evaluation

Ongoing evaluation of existing teachers differed little between public and private schools in our study. In several public and private schools the predominant theme seemed to be that principals had too many other responsibilities to devote significant attention to teacher evaluation, and there was a shortage of deputy administrators who could help with this critical aspect of instructional supervision. At one of the schools in our sample, Mashita Middle School, recent district budget cutbacks require subject department chairpersons to assume more teaching duties, leaving no time for observation and evaluation of other teachers. In the larger public schools, administrative tasks took most of the principals' time. In smaller private schools, especially those in low-income communities, fundraising and tuition negotiations with families experiencing financial difficulties was the most important consumer of principals' time.

In most public and private schools we studied, teachers were formally evaluated less than once a year and were rarely observed informally by principals (or other instructional supervisors) in addition to this formal evaluation. When they did take place, formal evaluations followed a similar ritualized pattern at a working-class public middle school like Mashita, at the Title I Multicultural Urban, at the reconstituted public Renaissance Middle School, at low-income Catholic schools like St. Felipe's or St. Milton's, at the for-profit Knuckleborough, and at St. Jeremy's, the lower-middle-income Lutheran school. At public schools, state law requires that probationary teachers receive a formal evaluation each year and that tenured teachers receive one every two years. At Catholic and Lutheran schools that attempt to follow a similar practice, however, we found that formal evaluations can occur as rarely as once every three years, if then.

These formal evaluations, in both public and some private schools, begin with a notification to the teacher that the principal plans to observe his or her classroom on a specific date and time. At that time, the teacher delivers a lesson prepared for this occasion. The principal observes the lesson, and makes check marks on a standardized form in which a range of teacher and classroom characteristics are listed. Following the observation, the teacher makes an appointment to meet with the principal, they review the evaluation, and the teacher signs a receipt for the form.

There were variations to this pattern. At the Liniers French School, although French government inspectors visit the school only once every two years to conduct a perfunctory formal evaluation of each teacher of the French curriculum, the school's instructional director evaluates all but the most senior teachers annually through a classroom visit and systematic review. At St. Donat's, the principal evaluates each teacher twice annually. At St. Barbara's, the principal conducts a formal evaluation of each teacher annually, even in the case of experienced teachers, and has attempted to deviate from the ritualized evaluation protocol common to the archdiocese and to public school districts. Several years ago, for example, she videotaped each teacher as part of the annual evaluation, and then watched the videotape with the teacher so that they could jointly explore strengths and weaknesses. Teachers objected to being videotaped, however, so the principal ceased doing so. She told us, however, that she hoped to resume the practice some time in the future.

Informal teacher evaluation

In low-income Catholic schools, we found principals themselves intimately involved in children's emotional development and disciplinary problems. These principals were in classrooms constantly, to resolve fights between children, to help settle unruly students, or to remove or counsel a student with a behavioral problem or an emotional difficulty. These principals, therefore, had a clear sense of teachers' strengths and weaknesses with regard to classroom management; but, even in these cases, principals did not have the time or inclination to address pedagogical or curricular issues.

Our discussions with principals revealed the extent to which, with these other pressures and obligations, they were able to keep academic performance a high priority in their evaluation of teachers. For example, the St. Milton's principal could not recall, for any classroom, the typical or average scores students obtained in the most recent Stanford Achievement Tests. This measure was not apparently an important consideration to be used in evaluating her teachers. This lack of attention to Stanford scores was in marked contrast to private schools in more affluent communities and to many public schools, where this measure of performance was widely known.

We asked one of these Catholic school principals to identify the "best" teachers in her school. The first teacher she identified "has a rapport with children so that when she teaches, she is firm. They know that they are loved and they are respected." A second "stimulates with creative materials that get the students to express themselves." And a third "has a very fatherly approach." In each of these cases, the teachers were also valued because they emphasized group work or "hands-on" activities, but their affective characteristics were paramount.

Other principals, in both public and private schools, made similar observations. We find this especially provocative because the scholarly literature increasingly claims that the most effective teachers (i.e., those who produce higher standardized test scores) are those teachers who themselves have higher scores on standardized tests, or who attended colleges whose students had higher average standardized test scores (e.g., Ballou and Podgursky 1997; Ehrenberg and Brewer 1995; Ferguson 1991). We know of no study that attempts to determine whether there is a correspondence between these measures and the characteristics of good teachers valued by the principals we interviewed, but we believe that such investigation should be a high priority for education research.

At several schools, while formal evaluations of teachers were rare and not meaningful, teachers reported receiving informal advice from their principals, advice they considered helpful. This advice generally followed a principal's visit to a classroom for some other purpose (to assist with a disciplinary problem, for example), and the principal incidentally noticed a pedagogical practice where different methods might be appropriate. Schools where teachers held the principal in high regard and expressed gratitude for such informal assistance included the public Mashita Middle and Multicultural Urban schools, quasi-public schools like Olympic, and private schools like St. Donat's, St. Barbara's, St. Felipe's, and Shalom Ieladim. At St. Milton's, the principal collects a sample of student work from each classroom each month, and from this work she makes a judgment about whether instruction is effective. In some of these schools, however, while the principals' advice was useful, without consistent follow-up it was not likely to make an important difference in instruction.

In large schools like Mashita Middle or in small private schools where the administrative and fundraising demands on the principals were more severe (especially the low-income Catholic schools), occasions for this sort of advice were rarer. At the small Olympic Charter, on the other hand, the principal visits each of the school's six classrooms two to three times each day, and frequently makes pedagogical suggestions to teachers. Several teachers reported that they felt these suggestions to be helpful, especially because many of them were experimenting with constructivist methods with which they had not previously been trained.

Several of the schools we observed have a mentor teacher program for beginning teachers. In some, like St. Felipe's and St. Jeremy's, the teachers reported getting little assistance from the mentor, although they were grateful for the fact that the mentor was available if needed. In one case about which we inquired, the mentor had observed a new teacher's class only twice during the course of the school year. How well a mentor system works is apparently dependent upon the personalities and inclinations of the teachers involved, not on strong direction from the principal. But at other schools, like Multicultural Urban, the mentor teacher system greatly supplements the principal's ability to advise new teachers and improve instruction. And at Olympic and Shalom Ieladim, the pairing of two teachers in a combined classroom creates a structure in which every teacher, new and old, can be complemented by another who may have different strengths and weaknesses.

With respect to evaluation, not only of teachers but of the entire school program, there were strong similarities between practices at Shalom Ieladim, Tatuna Point, and Olympic Charter. As noted in Chapter 1, in all three schools, parents complete extensive questionnaires each year evaluating their children's classrooms and teachers. Teachers also complete a questionnaire evaluating the principal. At Olympic, these evaluations are a very important quality control mechanism. One first-year teacher told us that she had spent the entire year dreading the parent evaluation process, because she had heard of veteran teachers crying when critical comments were returned.

Teacher retention and dismissal

The frequency of, and rationale behind, the voluntary departure or dismissal of school staff is another indication of the caliber of a school's instructional cadre and the standards used to monitor its performance. In schools where standards are clear, teachers who are not performing adequately or who do not fit in with the school's culture may leave voluntarily. This is especially true in public schools, where teachers have a right to request a transfer between schools. In other instances, principals find that they wish to fire a teacher whose performance has been disappointing or whose behavior is deemed inappropriate or worse.

An apparent distinction between public and private institutions lies in the power of private schools to fire teachers. The tenure system in public education makes the removal of a classroom instructor an arduous procedure, even in charter schools. No teacher, for example, has been fired from

Olympic because of poor performance. One teacher recently left voluntarily (or at least, by "mutual agreement"), transferring to a regular public school after a dispute over a new teacher hiring. This teacher's preference for the candidate to fill a position as her partner teacher was not honored by her peers or by the principal, who felt the nominee was not qualified to implement the constructivist philosophy. (At Olympic, teachers can veto a candidate for teacher-partner, but cannot alone select one.)[13]

The right to transfer to a regular school in the district is common in quasi-public charters like Olympic and Adams. On one occasion, a teacher assigned by the district was considered, after a trial period, to be unsuitable by the principal; however, a formal disciplinary process was not needed because the teacher could be transferred to another district school without penalty.

Because teachers can be more easily terminated at a private school, we would assume that the teacher evaluation process in private schools should have greater significance than in their public counterparts. However, we found little evidence that this is the case. For example, in one of the Catholic schools we observed, both the principal and vice principal stated that "I've never had to fire a teacher." In another Catholic school, two *new* instructors were asked to withdraw because, although offered several opportunities to improve their performance, they had continued to be evaluated as "substandard." This is precisely the same degree of control as in public schools, where all new teachers are effectively on probation for three years before being considered for tenure. It is relatively easy not to renew a public school teacher's probationary contract.

At St. Jeremy's Lutheran School, a teacher was fired for failing to comply with the school's core religious values and obligations. After parents complained that the instructor was not teaching any math, the school board launched an investigation. Less concerned with math problems than with the fact that the teacher had failed to fulfill a commitment to attend church services each Sunday, the school did not renew this teacher's contract. But this was an exception. Our observations led us to conclude that *experienced* teacher firing in private schools is a discretionary power that is seldom used, and it tends to be reserved for those rather extreme cases that could have also resulted in administrative action in a public school.

Teacher firings may be affected by current teacher labor market conditions: the shortage of qualified applicants may reduce a school's flexibility in firing inadequate teachers. When parents at the Liniers French School (which, due to its relatively low salary levels, may be especially affected by the California teacher shortage) complained about the lack of rigor in the English program's first-grade curriculum, the principal re-assigned the first-grade teacher to a kindergarten opening. On the other hand, when parents complained about two teachers in the *French* language program, and the principal, on the basis of his own review, concluded that the teachers were inadequate, the teachers were dismissed. The school's freedom to take this action may have stemmed from the fact that for each opening in its French language program it receives a great number of applications from French nationals certified by the French government to teach.

Within the Catholic school system, a reluctance to dismiss unsatisfactory teachers may be related less to the California teacher shortage and more to a bureaucratic disciplinary system. Catholic elementary schools are not formally accountable to the archdiocesan school department; in principle, each parish is independent in its control over its parish school. Yet the archdiocese in practice exercises strong control over parish elementary schools, coordinating curriculum, testing, budgeting, and, most dramatically, personnel policies. In cases where low-income schools receive an archdiocesan subsidy, the control is more formalized. Yet even at a suburban lower-middle-income school like St. Barbara's, while the archdiocesan supervisor insisted to us that her role in curriculum and personnel was only advisory, St. Barbara's principal stated that the archdiocese has "complete control. They monitor and they outline every move we make. We are always accountable to them."

Bureaucratic control of local Catholic elementary schools is clearest with regard to personnel policy. Archdiocesan policy is that its lawyers will represent any parish school whose administrators follow archdiocesan legal advice. None of the schools we observed were wealthy enough to consider functioning without this safety net and hiring their own attorneys, if need be. In practice, therefore, principals of Catholic schools we observed never took significant personnel actions without consulting first with their archdiocesan elementary school supervisor.

In general, the archdiocesan supervisors were conservative in their advice. While there is no tenure system in these Catholic schools, fear of lawsuits from discharged teachers is an ever-present motif guiding policy, resulting in an archdiocesan personnel handbook setting forth rules of progressive and consistent discipline for teachers that is nearly as restricting as the policies of unionized public school districts. Because, like public school principals, few Catholic school principals have the time (or experience) to invest in documenting past practice, progressive warnings, and consistent treatment, a potential discharge case is rarely approved by the archdiocese, because it rarely meets the standards of due process required by archdiocesan policies. Our interviews with Catholic school principals revealed that they approached unsatisfactory teachers in much the way public school principals do: either accept the situation, or engage in a policy of subtle harassment in hopes that the unsatisfactory teacher resigns.

For instance, the St. Felipe's school principal, after investigating several parent complaints, became dissatisfied with the instructional competence of a teacher. The principal, had not, however, documented a series of warnings and observations that would be necessary to meet the due process requirements of the personnel handbook. Instead, the principal eventually determined to relieve the teacher of her responsibilities for managing the student snack shop, a duty the principal knew the teacher enjoyed. The teacher became angered and told the principal she was quitting. The principal accepted the resignation on the spot, and, later, when the teacher calmed down and reconsidered, the principal got support from the archdiocese in refusing to permit the teacher to rescind her resignation.

Because the private schools we observed were mostly smaller than typical public schools, the faculties were more closely knit, and a policy of harassment might be more effective if the teacher no longer fit in with his or her colleagues. On the other hand, dissatisfied public school teachers can often utilize contractual rights to transfer to another school, while Catholic school teachers cannot. This lack of options may induce an unsatisfactory teacher to resist, to a greater extent than would be the case in a public school, pressures to leave.

In the case of more serious crimes, we found less reluctance on the part of Catholic schools than others to terminate a teacher's contract, whereas in public schools even these cases might result in grievances, hearings, and eventual monetary settlements. However, even in extreme cases, Catholic schools were more reluctant to take action than we anticipated. A St. Felipe's teacher, for example, was taunted by some high school students as she drove home. The teacher allegedly got out of her car and struck one with the heel of her shoe, causing injury. The teacher was arrested, but the archdiocese advised the St. Felipe's principal that she could take no action unless there was a conviction. Indeed, even though St. Felipe's teachers are on annual contracts, the school did not believe it could risk not renewing this teacher's contract while the criminal case was pending, for fear of a lawsuit.

During the course of these case studies, unmarried teachers became pregnant in two Catholic schools under observation. In each case, the principal and pastor thought the teacher should be fired and that the firing could be justified because the schools' standard employment contract includes a provision that teachers must lead a "moral life." In neither case did the school obtain archdiocesan approval to discharge the teacher.

Selection and retention: some observations

As with the other generalizations we examined, we found no clear distinctions between public and private schools in how they approached teacher personnel issues. While the Christian schools in our sample seemed to consider a candidate's religious behavior as an important qualification, all California schools — public and private alike — found their selection constricted by a statewide teacher shortage. We found a peer selection process effective, in both private and quasi-public schools, in assuring the selection of teachers whose pedagogical skills were consistent with school themes.

We found no school, public or private, where a formal evaluation system for teachers was meaningful or useful. However, we found several schools, public and private, where teachers welcomed the informal advice of their principals regarding their teaching styles and effectiveness. Some schools utilized parent surveys to evaluate teachers, and, in at least one of these cases, the parent surveys were taken seriously. In no case, public or private, did we find teachers evaluated, even in part, by test scores or other objective measures of their students' outcomes.

Most significantly, we found Catholic school procedures for terminating teachers to be nearly as cumbersome and bureaucratic as those in public schools. Contrary to our initial expectation, therefore, we do not conclude that public school systems can solve their serious problems in this area by adapting practices now in use in the Catholic schools.

In sum, despite the widely held view that private school teachers are likely to be "better" than public school teachers because of initial selection and fear of termination for poor performance, most private schools we observed were no more selective than public schools serving a similar socioeconomic group of students, nor were they likely to fire a teacher. If the teaching is better in one school than another, it does not seem to be attributable to private/public contractual differences.

Chapter 5

Similarity of Curriculum Materials

We generalized that *where private schools are academically successful, this success is accomplished with academic curricular materials that are not significantly different (in standard subjects) from curricular materials found in public schools.* We confirmed this generalization in some respects but not in all.

Formal curricular similarities

Overall, we did not detect great disparities among public and private schools in their formal academic curricula.

The Catholic schools we studied carefully followed a curriculum guide, published by the local archdioceses, for each grade level. It is published as a "Scope and Sequence" manual that specifies the number of minutes to be devoted to each academic subject each day.

In developing their curricula, the archdioceses relied heavily upon the state curriculum frameworks published by the California State Department of Education. As these frameworks also guide the curricula of most public schools, in this respect the curricula were strikingly similar. The similarity was reinforced because these Catholic schools administered the Stanford Achievement Test to students in each grade each year. Because this is the same test used by public schools in the local district, both public and Catholic schools would have to align their curricula with the Stanford Test if they wanted to assure high scores for their students.

The correspondence of the public and Catholic academic curricula was also necessary for two other reasons. First, the archdioceses probably did not have the resources to invest in developing an independent curriculum in as great detail as the California state frameworks. Second, Catholic schools could not afford to create a situation where misalignment of their curriculum with that of the public schools made transfers of students between the two systems more difficult. Not only do the Catholic schools want to recruit students from the public schools, but they want to preserve the flexibility to be able to expel (or counsel out) students who, for whatever reasons, may not be successful in the Catholic school system.

Perhaps the main difference between the curricular programs of Catholic and public establishments is the daily 45-minute period allotted to catechism and religious instruction. A lower-grade teacher, however, confesses that, under pressure, she sometimes cuts catechism to emphasize reading or math, thereby blurring even further the distinctions between public and private education:

> We're supposed to teach, theoretically, a certain amount of minutes of every subject every week, and it changes per grade. For example, [my grade] really concentrates on language arts, and you mostly teach language arts....What I end up doing, since religion is a 45-minute-a-day subject, if I need to cut into some subjects or not do a subject that day because we need to get to other things, I usually end up cutting out religion. I'll feel kind of guilty about it. This is a Catholic school. But then I'll do something at the end of the day, like if we say a prayer at the end of the day, and I'm like, all right, well we might not have read it in the religion book today, but we said a prayer today, and in all fairness, if I had to pick between something with language or math or cutting out religion, I'm going to cut out the religion, just because it's something you can go over again, but English and language and math are just so important.

The religious dimension of Shalom Ieladim Jewish School is a central aspect of its *raison d'être* as well as a key consideration for parents that enroll their children here, rather than in the high-quality public academic schools in its local district. It complements a rigorous general studies academic program with Judaic and Hebrew studies, and this religious instruction and related activities demand about 40% of students' time. The demands of this two-tiered curriculum on children, especially the youngest ones, are great. But in spite of the reduced time dedicated to the standard curriculum, a first-grade teacher remarks that "even though I'm only teaching 60 percent of the time for the general studies program, I think I still try to cram in 100 percent general studies education. I don't want the children to be missing anything." The general studies curriculum at Shalom Ieladim, in fact, follows the state academic framework closely.

In lower-income communities, we found supplementary reading programs for children whose reading skill was below the norm for their grade level in both public and private schools. At public Multicultural Urban, for example, the school purchases the "Reading Recovery" program. And although it was not used in schools observed for this report, we know that a growing number of schools throughout the nation are beginning to purchase the "Success for All" program with their Title I funds.

St. Felipe's and St. Milton's use a supplementary reading program called "Writing to Read," a computer-based phonics program sponsored by a foundation established by the local mayor. In return for an agreement to use this programmed reading instruction, low-income archdiocese schools receive a computer laboratory from the foundation, along with training for lab supervisors and teachers. There have been no scientific studies of the effectiveness of the Writing to Read program, nor of its relative value compared to the supplementary programs more commonly used in public schools.

Perhaps the only school that pursued a curricular program that significantly departed from the norm was St. Jeremy's Lutheran School. Every subject of the academic program was organized around religious themes. Even in this case, the Missouri Synod, like the Catholic archdiocese, attempts to align its curriculum guide with the California framework, but there is a distinct difference. As the school's principal explained, "kids are going to learn songs, they're going to do essays, they're going to do research papers," and they can do these things by learning church songs, by writing poems about their faith, and by doing research papers "from a religious perspective." Our classroom observations confirmed that academic instruction was frequently infused with a religious theme. The school, the principal noted proudly, "has promoted 'outcome-based education'...for 85 years. We want children to accept the Lord Jesus as their savior. And that's an outcome. We very much are interested in the outcome."

Similarities in curricula, differences in pedagogical skill

Nonetheless, and despite formal curricular similarities, there were significant differences in how the state frameworks were applied in the standard academic subjects. Several teachers we interviewed in lower- or middle-income Catholic and Lutheran schools were conscious of the extent to which they had not been trained, and had no access to training, in more advanced pedagogical techniques that they believed were frequently employed in public schools. Several who had undertaken public school observation visits said they felt unprepared to utilize manipulatives and to develop mathematical reasoning skills in lower-grade mathematics, approaches they saw in public schools and believed would be beneficial. They noted that public school classrooms they observed were more likely to utilize group work and cooperative learning techniques. They stated that they did not have well-stocked school libraries or the variety of literature available for young children to supplement the phonics texts the public schools made available, nor had they been trained to teach reading using such literature. Others noted that more computers were available in public school classrooms, a problem they felt adversely affected their ability to deliver an advanced and challenging curriculum. Several of these parochial school teachers reported that they sent their own children to public schools because their experience had taught them that the public curriculum was more advanced, both in the pedagogies employed in academic subjects and in the availability of non-academic extracurricular activities. These teachers, not surprisingly, lived in more affluent communities than the urban communities hosting the parochial schools at which they worked.

Of course, these teachers' admiration of the public school curriculum is not the same as a belief that average measured achievement is higher in public schools, and we of course do not draw any conclusions about typical public vs. private school instruction from these comments concerning a few comparisons of schools or classrooms. These parochial school teachers were likely invited to observe exemplary, not typical, public school classrooms. In our own public school observations for this report, we asked to see both exemplary and typical classrooms, and saw a wider range of instructional quality — some very good, some quite bad — than these teachers reported. In short, from the anecdotal data we collected, we cannot assert that private and public school instruction differed significantly.

In our school and classroom observations, we saw many attempts to develop new and more creative curricular approaches, in both public and private schools. In other schools, both public and private, we observed teaching that was simply textbook-driven. From our limited observations, however, the latter appeared to be more common in the lower-income religious private schools than in the public schools we studied.

At St. Barbara's, the Catholic school where academic goals are paramount for many participants, teacher creativity in delivering the curriculum is both enhanced and impeded by structures in place at the school. On the one hand, teachers regularly meet with other teachers and share curricular ideas, and try out on each other new lessons they have developed. Yet the school's teacher-pairing system also impedes creativity. Because the school has two classrooms in each grade, teachers at each grade level are expected to coordinate their lesson plans so that identical lessons are taught each day in both classrooms. While this system provides some support for teachers, it also limits experimentation and makes textbook-driven instruction more likely.

At Mashita Middle School, the policy is to organize all teachers into interdisciplinary teams in which teachers collaborate on thematic units in "schools within a school." While our case study was underway, one "pod" (as the teams are called) of teachers was focused on a Civil War project, in which literature, history, music, and art instruction were coordinated.

Yet as we conducted these case studies, another reality became clear: in schools without strong instructional leadership, variation in teaching between classrooms within schools can overwhelm the effects of any standardization of curricular materials used both within and among schools. While, for example, the urban religious schools we observed may have used the same science or social studies textbooks as did public schools (in some cases, they used discarded or out-of-print prior editions of these textbooks), if teachers instruct by asking students consecutively to stand, read a paragraph aloud from the textbook, and then sit down, academic outcomes will be poor regardless of how good standard curricular materials may be. In our classroom observations, we saw evidence of such uninspired teaching in private schools (including the most academically oriented of the Catholic schools, St. Barbara's), although this does not mean it is also not common in public schools as well — as noted, schools and classrooms selected for our observations were not designed to be representative.

On the other hand, we also saw examples of creative teaching in both public and private schools. From two years of classroom observations in these public and private schools, some exceptional teachers come to mind, mostly in public schools (again, this is not to suggest that they do not also exist in private schools). A public school teacher at Mashita Middle School excited a seventh-grade class, predisposed to be bored, with a lesson on the use of metaphor and simile — by playing the soundtrack from "Phantom of the Opera" and pausing after each verse to analyze the poetry. In another case, a fourth-grade public school teacher at the quasi-public Olympic Charter School taught a lesson on probability by describing the variety of colored socks she had at home in her sock drawer, and asking students to figure out which socks she was likely to wear to school the next day if she picked them when blindfolded. We were also impressed with the skill of a kindergarten teacher at St. Jeremy's Lutheran, who maintained her nurturing demeanor and instructional focus in the midst of the political maelstrom that engulfed the rest of the school.

Our conclusion, therefore, is that a superficial similarity of basic academic curricular materials in public and private schools does not necessarily entail a consistency of academic instruction. Public school teachers tend to be trained in more advanced pedagogies than most teachers in parochial schools in lower-income communities. As the previous chapter has shown, some of these public and private schools, however, are not structured to permit strong instructional leadership. Thus, there can be great variation in the delivery of the same curriculum within schools and within the nonprofit public and private sectors. If, by "similar curricula" we mean similar inconsistency in public and private schools, then our hypothesis may indeed be considered correct.

Chapter 6

Competitive Improvements

The final generalization we examined was that *private school innovations stimulate improved practices at the public schools with which they compete.* We did not confirm this hypothesis in our case studies, and we would certainly need to conduct many more cases to make a strong argument here. We did find two cases where school competition caused a school to improve or attempt to improve. In one case, it was a private school that came under competitive pressure from the public school system; in the other, a public school modified its program to compete with another public school. (Although while both schools were public, competition from an attractive private school might have had a similar effect.) Finally, we found one quasi-public school that aimed, as a central part of its mission, to influence nearby traditional neighborhood public schools to change. As a change agent, however, the quasi-public school failed miserably.

The private school that felt compelled to change because of competition from public schools was for-profit Knuckleborough. The school had previously attracted parents who found its smaller class sizes appealing, but then, as noted elsewhere in this report, in 1996-97 the state of California made substantial sums of money available to public schools for the purpose of reducing class sizes to 20 in grades K-3. Almost immediately, Knuckleborough saw its kindergarten applications plummet. When our case study concluded, the school's proprietor had not yet decided how to respond to this challenge, although her options were certainly limited, because Knuckleborough's low teacher salaries make it difficult to offset the loss of its class size advantage with an improvement in the quality of its instructional program.

The public school that changed was Mashita Middle School, located in a district which, for nearly two decades, has been under the supervision of a federal court desegregation order. One compliance policy implemented by the district has been the establishment of "magnet schools" throughout the city. Each magnet has an instructional theme, uses racial quotas to admit students who apply, and is designed to retain middle-class (white) families in the school district. An added inducement for families to apply for admission to magnet schools is that magnets provide home-to-school busing, whereas the district does not provide busing for neighborhood schools, even if, as in the case of Mashita Middle School, the school's catchment area is large. Thus, families concerned about their children's safety may apply to a magnet school to take advantage of the school bus service.

Less than five miles from Mashita Middle School is the Nosdod Middle Magnet School, with a curriculum built around a "math/science gifted" theme. The Mashita school principal estimates that, were it not for the Nosdod magnet school, white enrollment at Mashita Middle School would today be 25%, not 19%. She does not attribute the draw of the magnet school solely to its academic focus; she believes, for example, that parents are influenced by the fact that the Nosdod magnet is a new, attractive facility in a wealthy residential neighborhood in a separately incorporated suburban community, while Mashita has old-fashioned architecture (the school was built in 1928) and is closer to a major, run-down commercial thoroughfare.

Partly to compete for middle-class students who are attracted to Nosdod, Mashita Middle School was, during our study, constructing a "performing arts center." Mashita's principal hopes that, if the prospective performing arts center is recognized for high quality, sophisticated parents of adolescents will consider it as compelling as the math/science focus at the competing magnet school.

Mashita faculty also voted to embark on a series of school-based management reforms with support from a local grant from the Annenberg Foundation. Furthermore, Mashita, together with other schools in its high school cluster (which includes all middle and elementary schools that feed into the local public high school), has applied for a technology grant (Mashita has become the pilot demonstration school for the cluster). Important in the motivation is that this technology center will also help attract families who have other educational choices.

One of the primary goals of Olympic Charter is to influence nearby neighborhood schools to adopt its constructivist pedagogy. Yet Olympic has been entirely unsuccessful in having any influence on other public schools, to a considerable extent because, while it proclaims that it is distinguished from surrounding schools only by its constructivist pedagogy, in fact the economic and ethnic characteristics of its families set it dramatically apart from its neighbors.

Because the Olympic Charter School is also part of a district that has operated under a federal court desegregation order for nearly two decades, students apply for places set aside for children of their racial-ethnic group.

The purpose of these quotas is to guarantee a racially integrated school with sufficient numbers of nonminority children to make the school attractive to white families, thus discouraging further "white flight" from the school district. Within each quota group, students are assigned points (more points if a student's home school is overcrowded; more points if a sibling already attends the Olympic School), and then students are selected by lottery from those with the maximum number of points. This system, however, unintentionally assures that minority children who are selected to attend Olympic Charter will be less economically advantaged than typical minority children in the city, while white children who are selected to attend Olympic will be more typical of the city's white children. Thus, the economic status gap between Olympic's white and minority children could be greater than the status gap between white and minority children in the city as a whole. This outcome can occur because the growth of minority populations in minority communities has been such that the lowest-status minority children are more likely to attend overcrowded schools (and thus have extra points credited toward Olympic admission), whereas the schools that more advantaged minority students attend are less likely to be overcrowded. Schools in white communities are not overcrowded at all. One teacher estimates that, were it not for the existence of the Olympic Charter School, most of its white and Korean students would be attending private schools and some of its Latino students would be in parochial schools, but the African American students would mostly be attending their neighborhood public schools.

In 1995-96, the Olympic Charter School had enrollment that, as determined by quota, was 40% white, 21% Hispanic, 17% African American, 16% Asian, and 4% American Indian. In comparison, the neighborhood school with which the Olympic Charter School shares a campus was 3% white, 25% Hispanic, 71% African American, and 1% Asian. Olympic has had no discernible impact on its campus neighbor. Much to the frustration of Olympic's faculty, the neighboring school's teachers generally ignore invitations from the Olympic Charter School to observe at Olympic or to attend public events or demonstrations at the school. The schools were not even able to coordinate schedules to develop a common earthquake drill. At one point, tensions between the schools became so great that district officials intervened. Olympic's artist-in-residence had worked with parents and students to write a play, based on their own perceived reality, whose subject was two "fictional" schools that shared the same campus. The play was so offensive to teachers at the neighboring school that district officials solicited, and received, an apology from the Olympic principal.

Another illustration of the difficulty schools like Olympic have in stimulating imitation comes from a former Olympic teacher we interviewed who now teaches at an elementary school (with 53% black and 47% Hispanic student enrollment) in the heart of the city's most poverty-stricken community. Her departure from Olympic did not stem from disillusionment with its constructivism, and she remains a devotee of this pedagogy. In fact, in her regular school classroom, in marked contrast to the rest of her school, she emphasizes constructivist approaches she developed at Olympic — individualizing her curriculum, allowing children to work at their own pace, and rearranging her classroom to look more like a "living room" than the other classrooms in the school. But, she reports, while she expects her students at the end of this year to do "well" (i.e., average) in standardized testing in math, they can't read at grade level, have poor listening skills, and, although used to accepting commands, they are not, in contrast to Olympic School children, accustomed to asking questions. This is not to say that language arts results would remain poor if the entire school, rather than her isolated classroom, engaged in more student-centered learning, but it does suggest that duplicating the Olympic Charter School model is more complex than the school's promotional literature suggests.

One factor making the Olympic model difficult to imitate by other schools in its district, even if they became convinced of the value of constructivism, is the substantial additional funds parents have had to raise to supplement the school's public funding. These additional funds are used to hire resource teachers: a garden teacher, a team of drama teachers, a music teacher, an art teacher, a physical education teacher, and a computer technology consultant. Additional funds support the school library, purchase musical instruments for the music program, and finance special field trips — one class in the year before the case study took a $10,000 trip to an "outside science classroom" in the mountains. Funds are also given to each classroom for teachers to use in purchasing additional supplies; because of the school's constructivist approach, which places great emphasis on student "hands-on" activity, the Olympic School's instruction is more supplies-intensive than the thin school district allocation for materials would allow. In fact, the former Olympic teacher described above mentioned the lack of financial resources as an important impediment to her attempts to apply the constructivist approach to her classroom in her present school.

In sum, we saw a number of practices at schools in this study that might be worthy of imitation. In addition to the consistently creative teaching we saw at Olympic Charter, we observed the integration of academic and social services at Multicultural Urban and Renaissance; the consistent articulation of a high, if distant, academic goal at Multicultural Urban; the multidisciplinary pods at Mashita Middle School; the innovative curriculum at Adams Charter; the intimate personal involvement of the St. Felipe's principal in children's emotional lives; the priority on safety that parents find so attractive at Catholic and Lutheran schools, at Knuckleborough Urban Private School, and at Adams Charter; the co-optation of parents into the instructional program by the Liniers French School; and the extensive parent volunteerism at schools ranging from the public Tatuna Point and quasi-public Olympic Charter to schools where such volunteerism was mandated by contract.

We found no pattern, however, where private schools as a group had more to offer than public schools as a group or vice-versa. In many cases, the best practices we found at some public and private schools have limited transferability to schools, whether public or private, where the racial, ethnic, or economic backgrounds of families differed. But some of these best practices can be transferred, and perhaps they will be.

Chapter 7

Conclusions

Many analysts have claimed that private schools are more willing and able than public schools to respond to parents and to organize themselves, through more flexible curricula and teacher hiring/firing policies, for high academic achievement. But in our study of 16 schools, we found no evidence of such systematic differences.

Our study was not a random survey, and it was limited to a relatively small number of schools. Whatever lessons we draw in comparing types of schools must be qualified by this limitation. We have tried to be careful in drawing a variety of impressions to show that there is considerable variation among schools, both private and public. Given the restrictions of a small sample of 16 schools, we did our best to ensure that the schools we chose represented a typical range of different kinds of public and private schools. Such a sample can at least give us clues about how private and public schools may differ and how they may not.

Milton Friedman has argued that, by giving parents choice among all schools meeting minimum standards, parents could "express their views about schools directly, by withdrawing their children from one school and sending them to another, to a much greater extent than is now possible," and that "here, as in other fields, competitive private enterprise is likely to be far more efficient in meeting consumer demands than either nationalized enterprises or enterprises run to serve other purposes" (1955, 129).[14] John Chubb and Terry Moe (1990) compared public school organizations with their private counterparts, which are situated in an allegedly different institutional context. Private schools, controlled "indirectly—by the marketplace" serve as a contrast with public schools, controlled by democratic politics.[15] Because of the nature of these institutional settings — markets and politics — organization, they claim, tends to be very different in private and public schools. The main differences are that private schools have a great deal more discretion in terms of choosing what they do and how they do it, that they are less conflictual because of greater homogeneity of interests among parents, and that their teachers and administrators are not accountable to hierarchical public bureaucracies.

Our case studies suggest that these claims would be difficult to sustain in any careful comparison of private and public schools. We find that private schools operating in markets clearly have the prerogative to offer educational packages that vary considerably from typical public education. Yet, many private schools do not try to seek uniqueness by offering higher academic achievement than public schools serving a similar clientele. Rather, these private schools are more likely to offer more "order" to families seeking a safer, more disciplined environment, or a religious mission. In a few cases, private schools offer a particular method of teaching (such as a constructivist approach) that may be available in some but not all public schools, or private schools may sometimes offer an even more specific educational product (such as dual-language immersion). But for many if not most private schools, our observations suggest that economist Byron Brown was mostly right when he stated that private schools cannot risk offering even modest departures from the "tried and true" academic packages offered by public schools.

In assessing what the public education sector can learn from the nonprofit private education sector, our study therefore points away from the arguments that public schools need to adopt the greater accountability to parents and the flexibility in hiring and firing teachers characteristic of private schools. These may be good policies for all schools to follow, but public schools with students from upper-middle-class families are just as likely to be accountable to their parents as private schools serving the same clientele. Similarly, we found no evidence that private schools evaluated teachers more often or with greater stringency than did public schools.

We learned something about the effects, and possible effects, of competition between schools. We observed private schools that drew students away from public schools because they offered an educational package that differed from the public package in that school district. We observed private schools that specialized in religious education, along with the "moral-religious-disciplined" environment that such education implies. Parents placing a high value on a religious educational environment or on the greater safety and discipline it promises tend to send their children to religious schools. Obviously, religious education would not be an option for public schools, but a highly disciplined environment that included uniforms and tough behavior codes could be.

The private (and public charter) schools we observed that offered a unique academic approach (like dual-language immersion, or construct–ivism) both catered to relatively affluent and/or highly educated parents.

These schools clearly met a need that neighborhood public schools did not fulfill. But we also had the opportunity to note the impact on a neighborhood school that competition from one with a unique academic focus can have. In this case, there were some healthy consequences of the competition, but some very deleterious ones as well.

Public schools that are poorly run can learn their most important lessons from well-run public *and* private schools, but we have uncovered no evidence that these lessons will be diffused through increased market accountability. We suspect there may be two reasons for this. First, private schools do not appear to be inherently more effective than public, hence more private schools in an education market will not necessarily mean more good models. Second, although some private (and public choice) schools have unique academic programs, some private schools in our sample appear to compete for students mainly by offering nonacademic products (religion, safety, or a unique environment) that differentiate them from their public counterparts in the same market. So the lesson that might be learned is how to differentiate a product mix, rather than deliver more academic learning.

Some interesting differences arose between the findings of our study and the conclusions of Bryk, Lee, and Holland in their highly regarded *Catholic Schools and the Common Good* (1993), a comparison of Catholic and public schools. In some respects, of course, our work is not comparable. Bryk, Lee, and Holland's study was of secondary schools, whereas this report concerns only elementary schools. Their fieldwork took place in "good" Catholic high schools, whereas we, while not excluding schools of exceptional quality, made no effort to select schools on that basis.

Like Bryk and his colleagues, we found Catholic school faculties with an educational philosophy that went beyond academic concerns to issues of social justice and moral behavior. But we found such sense of purpose also in some public schools we observed, and in some non-Catholic private schools as well. Bryk, Lee, and Holland's description of schools "organized around strong normative principles," combining a "strong emphasis on academic work with a caring ethos that demands personal responsibility," with a set of "humanistic beliefs and social principles" (p. 327) characterized, to some extent, the Catholic elementary schools we observed, but could equally characterize the faculties of Multicultural Urban and Olympic public schools, could characterize some administrators and teachers at Mashita, and could also characterize the leaders of non-Catholic private schools like Shalom Ieladim.

Our primary difference with Bryk and his colleagues, however, stems from their observation that parents in Catholic schools, to a greater extent than in other schools, participate in a "voluntary community" where they "ease the work of the school staff by ensuring that students attend regularly, do their homework, and adhere to the school's behavioral standards," and that their relationship to school staffs can be characterized as a "trust relationship" (p. 305-6). There were certainly parents with whom we spoke, and about whom the faculty we interviewed spoke, to whom such characterizations applied, but we did not observe these qualities to be particularly more frequent in the private schools or in the Catholic schools in our sample. Rather, in this respect as in so many others, the social, cultural, and economic backgrounds of the parents and the community in which the school was located seemed to be the main determinant of variation, much more so than a school's public or private character or, within the latter group, whether it was religious or secular. Within these particular communities, the similarities between schools and the problems they confronted overwhelmed the differences.

Appendix A: Case Study Descriptions

The 16 schools examined in this study are located in the Los Angeles, San Francisco, or San Jose metropolitan areas. In each case, interview subjects were assured anonymity for themselves and their institutions; therefore, the names of the schools are pseudonyms. Each school is described below, followed by the name of the primary author(s) who observed the school; conducted interviews with administrators, teachers, and parents; and wrote a report summarizing conclusions.

In addition, **Table A-1** classifies each school studied by the predominant socioeconomic characteristics of the children who attend and by whether the school is private-religious, private-non-sectarian, private-for-profit, public-neighborhood, or public-choice. The schools in the table are identified by the numbers used in the descriptions below.

1. Adams Charter Middle School. A public charter school started by parents in 1994, Adams' charter requires that the school abide by all provisions of the California Education Code, giving it many characteristics of a public school. On the other hand, parents supplement the public budget with monthly "pledges" of $85; the average annual pledge is $702 per child. Thus, while we categorize this as one of the public schools in our study, it could arguably be considered a private school. The school is located in a suburban community, and its 75 seventh- and eighth-grade students are mostly from upper-middle-class families. Student ethnicity reflects that of the community: 85% of Adams' students are white, 14% are Latino, and one student is "other." This case study was authored by Paula Louzano.

2. Ayacucho Elementary School. A Title I public elementary school (whole school), Ayacucho enrolls approximately 450 students in grades K-5. It is located in a low-income urban area that is on the outskirts of one of the nation's most affluent suburban school districts. About half of the school's students are Latino, and a small percentage are Asian or African American. Ayacucho operates a bilingual as well as an English educational program at each grade level. This case study was authored by Martin Carnoy.

3. Knuckleborough Private School. Housed in a three-building complex in the heart of a low- to middle-income central city neighborhood, this nearly 30-year-old for-profit private K-8 school of 360 students is now owned and operated by the founder's widow and children. Students come from middle-class single or two-parent working families who pay $5,000 in annual tuition, plus additional fees for extended care (from 7:00 a.m. to 6:30 p.m.). The student body is predominantly white, but not exclusively so; the regular teaching staff is entirely white. The school has small classes (there are two classroom teachers for each grade, plus six school-wide resource teachers) and low salaries (average teacher salary of $24,000), with consequent teacher turnover exceeding 40% a year. Students, however, tend to remain at

Table A-1: School case studies, by predominant student socioeconomic status and race/ethnicity

	Low income	Lower-middle income	Middle income	Affluent
Public:				
Neighborhood	2, 7, 9	6		16
Choice - charter	5		8	1
Private:				
Religious	13, 15	11, 12	14	10
Nonsectarian				4
For profit			3	

	Mostly African American	Mostly Latino	Mostly white	No predominant race/ethnicity
Public:				
Neighborhood		2, 6	16	7, 9
Choice - charter		5	1	8
Private:				
Religious	13, 15	11, 12	10, 14	
Nonsectarian			4	
For profit			3	

the school, and many spend a full nine years at Knuckleborough. There is no parent organization, and the school philosophy does not emphasize parent involvement, especially in the classroom, so the owner-operators of the school maintain tight control of the institution. This case study was authored by Diana Rhoten.

4. Liniers French School. This private independent school of 350 students provides an immersion-based bilingual and multicultural education to students from pre-kindergarten through 7th grade. The student body is 61% French, 32% American, and 7% international. Located in an affluent suburb of a major city, the annual tuition rate is approximately $9,500. The school is accredited by the French Ministère de l'Éducation Nationale as well as by the California Association of Independent Schools. In the last few years, a Chinese section has been added to the school as well. This case study was authored by Gayatri Sethi and Martin Carnoy.

5. Madison Charter School. Because it had consistently produced the lowest achievement scores in its district, Madison was selected by the county's board of supervisors to become a charter school in 1994. Of the nearly 600 K-6 students who attend Madison, 89% are Latino, and most of these live in a low-income community where most residents are originally from Mexico. From the neighboring predominantly white, affluent community, relatively few children attend Madison. As a charter school, Madison differs from regular public schools in some important respects: there is a 210-day school year instead of the standard 180; parents must sign a contract to volunteer in the school for four hours a month; there is a preschool on the premises, although preschool enrollment is low because fees are charged on a sliding scale that many parents consider too expensive; and the school offers a fully operational health clinic. This case study was authored by Zoe Anne Gillett.

6. Mashita Middle School. A public middle school of 1,700 students, Mashita's enrollment has historically been drawn mostly from families of longshoremen and other port workers who dominate its harbor community. School officials are troubled by a community culture that, despite the impact of containerization on longshore jobs, assumes that good jobs will be available to young people who don't have a good education. The mostly stable working-class community is undergoing demographic change as well: 19% of the students are limited-English proficient. Of the total student body, 62% are Latino, 13% are African American, and 21% are nonminority whites. This case study was authored by Richard Rothstein.

7. Multicultural Urban Public School. In a lower- to middle-income area of a major city, Multicultural Urban Public School enrolls 710 K-5 students, three-quarters of whom are eligible for free or reduced-price lunches; half are limited-English proficient. A district-wide desegregation court order requires that no more than 45% of the school's students can be of one racial or ethnic group. Thus, Multicultural is roughly 31% Chinese, 28% Latino, 15% African American, 12% Filipino, 9% "other nonwhite," and 4% "other white." Because of its Spanish and Chinese bilingual programs, however, many classrooms do not reflect the school's diversity. This case study was conducted during the first year of California's state-sponsored class-size reduction initiative, and Multicultural was able suddenly to reduce class sizes to 20 in the primary grades. The school also attempts to integrate health, mental health, social, educational, and other support services, including financial and legal services for parents and health and immigration services for the whole family. A neighborhood community center works collaboratively with the school to provide parenting classes, adult literacy classes, and child care. This case study was authored by Sandra Stein.

8. Olympic Charter School. Originally a magnet school, this K-5 public school of 385 students applied for and received charter status, although it remains financially fully integrated with its urban school district. Charter status makes more explicit the constructivist educational philosophy around which the magnet was initially organized. Olympic is heavily dependent on parent and corporate fundraising to supplement the per-pupil allotment the school receives from the school district. The relative advantages of its parent pool, compared to other schools in its urban, mostly low-income district, are illustrated by the fact that it hosts an annual parent fundraising dinner where tickets are $100 a plate. This case study was authored by Richard Rothstein.

9. Renaissance Middle School. Renaissance is a public school that, because of consistently low student achievement, was "reconstituted" by the district superintendent in 1994 with an entirely new faculty and staff. Located in a low-income community with substantial public housing, Renaissance's student body is 31% African American, 22% Chinese, 16% Latino, 14% Filipino, 14% other minority groups, and 2% other white. This demographic mix is typical of the district; what is atypical is the source of this diversity. While other schools in the district achieve their multiethnic composition through a desegregation decree and busing, Renaissance students arrive on foot, and they reflect the neighborhood's demography. Of the school's 450 sixth- through eighth-grade students, 32% are limited-English proficient; over 75% qualify for free or reduced-price lunches; and 17% are classified as eligible for special education. This case study was authored by Matt Kelemen and Jennifer O'Day.

10. Shalom Ieladim Jewish School. Founded in 1990, this private day school of grades K-5 serves families of reform, reconstructionist, conservative, orthodox, and unaffiliated Jewish backgrounds. It is located in, and draws its students primarily from, an affluent suburb, and has an annual tuition rate of $6,950; the Jewish Community Federation provides an additional subsidy of $850 per student per year. In an attempt to remain diverse, the school allocates about 20% of its budget to need-based scholarships for those who cannot afford full tuition. About one-quarter of the school's 150 students have emigrated from Israel or Russia. Most parents are professionals in the service or technology industries. All students are Jewish, but some academic teachers are not. The school's academic program is complemented with Judaic and Hebrew studies. This case study was authored by Luis Benveniste.

11. St. Barbara's Catholic School. Located in an inner suburb of a major U.S. city, this K-8 private school of 600 students (with two classrooms per grade) has a competitive admissions process, and each year tests nearly twice the number of kindergarten applicants as there are spaces available. Transfer students to fill vacancies are also admitted, provided they test at "grade level." A neighboring public school reflects the surrounding community: 92% Latino enrollment and 64% free- or reduced-price-lunch eligible. Because of its selective admissions process, St. Barbara's enrollment is somewhat less impoverished and minority than this surrounding community. The school is operated directly by St. Barbara's parish, whose pastor hires the principal. She is the only member of a religious order still on the faculty. The school provides a before- and after-school day care program, and also staggers the daily schedule for primary students to provide smaller classes and more intensive reading instruction at the beginning and end of each school day. This case study was authored by Richard Rothstein.

12. St. Donat's Catholic School. A nine-classroom, 230-student K-8 school, St. Donat's is operated by a Dominican Sisters order in conjunction with the local archdiocese, although the school is owned by St. Donat's Parish. The faculty consists of three Dominican nuns and eight lay teachers, with another Dominican as part-time special needs coordinator. Enrollment is 69% Latino, 13% Asian, 11% white, and 7% African American. Most parents work in service jobs like waitressing, janitorial services, cooking, accounting, insurance, and minibus driving. The majority of St. Donat's families have two wage earners; about one-quarter are single-parent families. Annual tuition is $2,350. With an operating cost of $2,800, the school devotes great effort to fundraising events and seeking foundation grants. In a few cases, tuition reductions have been granted for needy families. Rising real estate values in the surrounding community result in continuing enrollment loss, as the kinds of families who traditionally enrolled their children move away. This case study was authored by Luis Benveniste.

13. St. Felipe's Catholic School. Also operated by the Dominican Sisters for the local parish, St. Felipe's is a K-8 inner-city school of 290 students, with one classroom in each grade. The principal, a Dominican, is the only member of a religious order on the faculty. St. Felipe's Parish experienced serious rioting earlier in this decade; since that time, the community has changed rapidly, from mostly African American to mostly Latino. Enrollment, drawn almost entirely from the surrounding parish, is now 70% African American and 30% Latino; about half the students are non-Catholic. Nearly 40% live with single parents (most of whom are employed), and another 7% live with grandparents. St. Felipe's offers a morning care program for children whose parents work, beginning at 6:00 a.m. (and serving breakfast), and an after-school program until 6:00 p.m. Tuition is $2,500 a year, with a discounted plan available for parents who engage in fundraising activities. The archdiocese provides 26 students with scholarships of $600 each. St. Felipe's students average close to the second stanine on national norm-referenced tests. This case study was authored by Richard Rothstein.

14. St. Jeremy's Lutheran School. Located in the same inner suburban community as St. Barbara's Catholic School, St. Jeremy's Lutheran was operated by a parish that, consistent with Missouri Synod policy, had complete autonomy from higher church bodies. This K-8 school of 206 students (in one classroom per grade level) was operated by a parish-elected board that selected the principal, interviewed teacher candidates, and reviewed all major curricular and other school policies. As the community changed to become predominantly Latino, few parish families any longer had school-age children; only eight parishioner children were enrolled during the 1996-97 school year. Students were majority Spanish-surnamed, reflecting nonparishioner enrollment from the surrounding community. Nonetheless, the school retained a strong religious focus. One of the nine classroom teachers was an ordained Lutheran minister; others were graduates of the Missouri Synod's Concordia College system or were required to have equivalent religious training. While this case study was being conducted, St. Jeremy's was riven by policy disputes between the board, the pastor, the principal, and the faculty. Unable to resolve these, the school closed at the end of the 1997-98 school year. This case study was authored by Richard Rothstein.

15. St. Milton's Catholic School. Another K-8 school operated by the Dominican Sisters in the same riot-impacted community where St. Felipe's Catholic School is located, St. Milton's School differs in that its 220 students (in one classroom per grade level) are not drawn primarily from the surrounding community. Many come from families who moved to more suburban communities as the parish changed, but who send their children back to the parish school that the parents themselves attended. Still, there is high attrition, and, with a target class size of 35 in all grades, only six 8th graders last year had been in the school since kindergarten. The 60% of the students who are African American come mostly from families with origins in Belize or in French-speaking Louisiana, in contrast to more typical African American families with origins in the Southeastern U.S. Based on parish demographics in the 1990 Census, the archdiocese subsidizes the school, and tuition ranges from $1,625 for parishioners' children to $1,975 for non-Catholic students. The principal also engages in extensive tuition negotiations with families in financial difficulty, and fundraising is a major focus. This case study was authored by Richard Rothstein.

16. Tatuna Point Elementary School. A public elementary school of 560 K-6 students, Tatuna Point is located in a high-income suburban community where many parents are professionals, businesspeople, and corporate executives. Parents logged a total of 8,000 volunteer hours in the school last year. Enrollment is 78% white and 20% Asian. Average test scores are above the 90th percentile on nationally normed standardized tests, and most children are expected eventually not only to attend college but to attend elite institutions of higher education. A parent-run educational foundation raised $130,000 in the last year; the funds were used to hire two full-time resource teachers and six part-time paraprofessionals to supplement the regular staff hired from district funds. The PTA donated an additional $50,000 for computers and playground equipment. This case study was authored by Luis Benveniste.

Endnotes

1. A few notes about the schools studied: (1) the sample of eight public elementary schools includes three middle schools, but the private school sample includes none, because middle schools are rare in the private sector; thus, our sample of eight private schools includes both the primary and middle grades; (2) three of the eight public schools are charter schools; they might more accurately be described as either "quasi-public" or "quasi-private" schools; and (3) although this report aims to enlighten the debate about what public schools can learn from the private *nonprofit* sector, one of the private schools on which we report is a family-owned, for-profit institution; we included it because we believe this school can also shed some light on the research question.

2. This working theory is described more fully in earlier papers related to this project. See, for example, Abelmann and Elmore (1999) and Carnoy, Benveniste, and Rothstein, (1999). Each of the interviewers worked from the same set of protocols, one for teachers, one for administrators, and one for parents. The questions were organized around this theory of accountability.

3. Chubb and Moe (1990) and others who champion markets in education explicitly assume that both public and private schools are highly aligned in one sense: they adhere closely to external accountability systems. Public schools are aligned with bureaucratic goals, while private schools are aligned with clients' (parents') taste for academic achievement. Chubb and Moe implicitly assume that private schools are more likely to have aligned accountability (coherence between parents'/teachers' expectations, internalized notions of accountability, and the school's formal accountability system) in cases where markets reward academically excellent schools with more students. Concurrently, Chubb and Moe and many other private school advocates assume that public schools are not organized to maximize achievement. In public schools, they believe, bureaucratic goals conflict with teachers' notions of good teaching, conflict with parents' demands for academic excellence, and produce formal accountability systems unrelated to maximizing academic achievement.

4. Because private schools in low-income communities generally cannot support themselves with tuition alone, private schools serving these populations tend to be religious schools operating with some form of church subsidy, whether in the form of school buildings, low salaries for religious faculty, or administrative and support services.

5. The religious schools we studied also use a "scrip" program as a fundraising device. Under such a program, families purchase scrip that can be redeemed for purchases at local stores. The merchants who agree to accept this scrip then donate a small percentage of these sales to the school.

6. As we describe below, this school closed after the 1997-98 school year.

7. The school benefits from a grant from the Annenberg Foundation, which underwrites the costs of several reform initiatives.

8. In 1998, California changed policy and prohibited most bilingual instruction. We have not revisited Multicultural since that time to assess how it has adapted to this prohibition, and so have no insight into whether this new policy has caused a reduction in parental participation. A recent court decision has prohibited the continuation of the district's quota system for integration as well, so Multicultural's character may change in the near future.

9. We frequently heard references to gang problems at neighborhood public schools. These references, while accurate, may have been somewhat exaggerated. Nonetheless, parent perceptions that parochial schools were "safer" may not truly reflect only concerns about safety. The actual incidents of fighting and violence may not have been that different in parochial and public schools in the same neighborhood. Rather, when some parents referred to parochial schools' "safety," it was sometimes a euphemism for traditionally ordered and disciplined. Student uniforms and quiet order may create an atmosphere less welcoming to violent behavior, even if actual numbers of violent incidents don't differ very much from neighboring schools where such symbols of order are not present.

10. There is a common misunderstanding in our public debates that, if schools performed adequately, all students would read "at grade level." Yet "grade level" is conventionally defined as the point at which 50% of all students are above and 50% are below. If schools were all equally effective, and if children's achievement reflects, to some extent, what they learn at home and in their communities, it is to be expected that children from more disadvantaged backgrounds would be more likely to read below grade level and children from more advantaged backgrounds would be more likely to read above. For a fuller discussion of this point, see Rothstein (1998), pp. 93-100.

11. In only one of the Catholic schools we studied — the more middle-income St. Barbara's — was preparation for competitive admission tests for Catholic secondary

schools an important school goal. In the others, students took these tests, but generally then attended either the less-selective Catholic high schools or public high schools. In all the Catholic schools we observed, however, there were at least some parents for whom high scores on secondary school admission tests were an important goal, and this attention assured that an academic focus remained a serious, if not the primary, school characteristic. Thus, if these low-income Catholic schools do not reach high academic standards, we do not necessarily conclude that this is due solely to the fact that academic goals are merely second to religious goals.

12. We did not observe a similar concern at St. Jeremy's Lutheran School and, indeed, were surprised at the lack of sophistication about contemporary social issues in some respects.

13. This teacher was also the only African American teacher at Olympic, which lies in a district where there are substantial numbers of African American teachers. We did not investigate this aspect of the teacher's departure, and raise it here only because it was an aspect to which our interviewees, troubled by whether it was coincidental or reflected an institutional problem, frequently referred.

This aspect might fruitfully be examined, perhaps to determine if something about the "constructivist" teaching approach attracts fewer African American teachers to Olympic, or if African American teachers feel less comfortable in a school dominated by a philosophy associated with "offbeat" middle-class white professional parents, or if these parents or the other teachers themselves are not welcoming to African American teachers, or if the relative absence of such teachers is simply accidental. There is also a possibility, unconfirmed, that there lies a danger in a hiring process that emphasizes peer evaluations if this process institutionalizes an informal and exclusive network.

At Ayacucho Elementary School, the two African American teachers on the faculty were those least sympathetic to a "constructivist" teaching approach. These upper-grade teachers had high standards and emphasized basic skills to a much greater extent, and they frequently complained to other teachers that children came to their classes academically unprepared. As at Olympic, there was no obvious racial aspect to this difference in style, although our interviewees were aware of, and somewhat troubled by, the apparent racial pattern.

Studying racial or ethnic patterns in school types and pedagogies was not part of our research design, and we do not know if these speculations would or would not lead to productive areas of inquiry in the other schools we observed.

14. For Friedman, public schools are inefficient because nothing *makes* them be efficient, at least in terms of delivering the kinds of services that parents want. Public schools do not have to compete on the same ground with other schools that might deliver more and better education. And with a "monopoly" in neighborhood education, public schools are likely to produce education in a way that serves purposes other than parent wishes.

15. Although this "carries no value judgment," because "all organizations of any size are in some sense bureaucratic" and all government agencies are political, Chubb and Moe claim that the "public school system suffers from very serious problems along both these dimensions....Its bureaucracy problem is not that the system is bureaucratic at all, but that it is too heavily bureaucratic — too hierarchical, too rule-bound, too formalistic — to allow for the kind of autonomy and professionalism schools need if they are to perform well. Its political problem is not that it is subject to any sort of democratic politics, but that the specific political institutions by which the schools are governed actively promote and protect this over-bureaucratization" (p. 26).

Bibliography

Abelmann, Charles, and Richard Elmore. 1999. "When Accountability Knocks, Will Anyone Answer?" Cambridge, Mass.: Consortium for Policy Research in Education (mimeo).

Ballou, Dale, and Michael Podgursky, 1997. *Teacher Pay and Teacher Quality.* Kalamazoo, Mich.: W.E. Upjohn Institute for Employment Research.

Brown, Byron. 1992. "Why Governments Run Schools." *Economics of Education Review*, Vol. 11, No. 4, pp. 287-300.

Bryk, Anthony S., Valerie E. Lee, and Peter B. Holland. 1993. *Catholic Schools and the Common Good.* Cambridge, Mass.: Harvard University Press.

Carnoy, Martin, Luis Benveniste, and Richard Rothstein. 1999. *Public and Private School Effectiveness: A Reappraisal.* Berkeley, Calif.: Policy Analysis of California Education (PACE).

Chubb, John, and Terry Moe. 1990. *Politics, Markets and America's Schools.* Washington, D.C.: Brookings Institution.

Coleman, James S., Thomas Hoffer, and Sally Kilgore. 1982. *High School Achievement.* New York: Basic Books.

Ehrenberg, Ronald G., and Dominic J. Brewer. 1995. "Did Teachers' Race and Verbal Ability Matter in the 1960's? Coleman Revisited." *Economics of Education Review,* Vol. 14, pp. 291-99.

Ferguson, Ronald F. 1991. "Paying for Public Education: New Evidence on How and Why Money Matters." *Harvard Journal on Legislation,* Vol. 28, pp. 465-98.

Friedman, Milton. 1955. "The Role of Government in Education." In Robert Solo, ed., *Economics and the Public Interest.* New Brunswick, N.J.: Rutgers University Press.

Peterson, Paul E. 1998. *An Evaluation of the New York City School Choice Scholarships Program: The First Year.* Washington, D.C.: Mathematica Policy Research.

Ravitch, Diane. 1974. *The Great School Wars: New York City, 1805-1973.* New York: Basic Books.

Rothstein, Richard. 1998. *The Way We Were? The Myths and Realities of America's Student Achievement.* New York: Century Foundation.

Rouse, Cecilia Elena. 1997. *Private School Vouchers and Student Achievement: An Evaluation of the Milwaukee Parental Choice Program.* Working Paper No. W5964. Cambridge, Mass.: National Bureau of Economic Research.

Scott, W. Richard, and John Meyer. 1988. "Environmental Linkages and Organizational Complexity: Public and Private Schools." In Thomas James and Henry Levin, eds., *Comparing Public and Private Schools.* Philadelphia, Pa.: Falmer Press.

Talbert, Joan. 1988. "Conditions of Public and Private School Organization and Notions of Effective Schools." In Thomas James and Henry Levin, eds., *Comparing Public and Private Schools.* Philadelphia, Pa.: Falmer Press.

Witte, John F. 1996. "School Choice and Student Performance." In Helen F. Ladd, ed., *Holding Schools Accountable.* Washington, D.C.: Brookings Institution.

About the authors

RICHARD ROTHSTEIN is a research associate of the Economic Policy Institute, a contributing editor of *The American Prospect,* and an adjunct professor of public policy at Occidental College in Los Angeles. He is the author of *The Way We Were? The Myths and Realities of America's Student Achievement* (Century Foundation Press 1998); *Where's the Money Going? Changes in the Level and Composition of Education Spending 1991-96* (Economic Policy Institute 1997); *Where's the Money Gone? Changes in the Level and Composition of Education Spending 1967-91* (with Karen Hawley Miles; Economic Policy Institute 1995); and co-editor (with Edith Rasell) of *School Choice: Examining the Evidence* (Economic Policy Institute 1993).

MARTIN CARNOY is professor of education and economics at Stanford University. Before coming to Stanford, he was a research associate at the Brookings Institution. He is the author of *Schooling and Work in the Democratic State* (with Henry Levin); *Faded Dreams: The Economics and Politics of Race in America;* and, most recently, *Sustaining Flexibility: Work, Family and Community in the Information Age,* to be published by Russell Sage. He has also written extensively on the impact of privatization through voucher plans in Chile, Europe, and the United States. He is currently researching educational improvement efforts in Texas and Kentucky.

LUIS BENVENISTE is an education specialist at the World Bank. He has conducted research on formal and informal school accountability mechanisms in public and private schools for the Consortium for Policy Research in Education; his recent work has focused on the politics of student achievement testing in Argentina, Chile, and Uruguay. He has served as a consultant for a wide variety of international education projects in Bolivia, Chile, Jamaica, and Mexico. Mr. Benveniste holds a Ph.D. in international comparative education from Stanford University.

Questions or comments about this report may be directed to the authors at:

rothstei@oxy.edu
carnoy@leland.stanford.edu
luisb@leland.stanford.edu

About EPI

The Economic Policy Institute was founded in 1986 to widen the debate about policies to achieve healthy economic growth, prosperity, and opportunity.

Today, America's economy is threatened by increasing inequality. Expanding global competition, changes in the nature of work, and rapid technological advances are altering economic reality. Yet many of our policies, attitudes, and institutions are based on assumptions that no longer reflect real world conditions.

With the support of leaders from labor, business, and the foundation world, the Institute has sponsored research and public discussion of a wide variety of topics: trade and fiscal policies; trends in wages, incomes, and prices; the causes of the productivity slowdown; labor-market problems; education; rural and urban policies; inflation; state-level economic development strategies; comparative international economic performance; and studies of the overall health of the U.S. manufacturing sector and of specific key industries.

For additional information, contact EPI at 1660 L Street, NW, Suite 1200, Washington, DC 20036, (202) 775-8810, or visit www.epinet.org.

About The Nonprofit Sector Research Fund

The Nonprofit Sector Research Fund awards research grants and organizes convenings to expand knowledge of the nonprofit sector and philanthropy, improve nonprofit practices, and inform public policy related to nonprofits. Established at The Aspen Institute in 1991, the Fund seeks to enhance both the quantity and quality of nonprofit research by increasing the legitimacy and visibility of nonprofit scholarship; encouraging new investment in sector research; supporting the exploration of tough, neglected questions; and enlarging the number of creative scholars and practitioners interested in pursuing nonprofit studies.

The Nonprofit Sector Research Fund's programs are supported by the Carnegie Corporation of New York, The Ford Foundation, William Randolph Hearst Foundation, The James Irvine Foundation, W.K. Kellogg Foundation, Charles Stewart Mott Foundation, The David and Lucile Packard Foundation, and others.